Student Worktext Level B

A Reason For Spelling® Student Worktext - Level B
2nd Edition

EAN#: 978-1-58938-271-8
ISBN#: 1-58938-271-4
TL#: SPSWTB2019WC

Published by Concerned Communications, LLC
P.O. Box 1000, Siloam Springs, AR 72761

Authors: Rebecca Burton, Eva Hill, Leah Knowlton, Kay Sutherland
Illustrations: James McCullough & Mark Decker

Phonics Section
Day 1 through Day 31

In this **Student Worktext, Level B,** the Phonics Section (yellow edge tabs) offers a series of **fun activities** based on **partner letters** and **sounds** to help strengthen a student's phonics skills. If you do one page per day, you can complete this section in approximately seven weeks.

If you are using a "stand-alone" Phonics program, this section can simply be used for review and reinforcement.

A Poetry Connection

Name ______________________________

The Universe God Made

God made a lot of round things,
Like the earth and shining stars,
The sun, and moon, and planets;
Venus, Mercury, Saturn, and Mars.

He hung them all up in the sky,
To show His love and care;
So when I see their shining light,
I know that God is there.

Fill in the letter that comes between the given letters:

1. a ___ c x ___ z t ___ v
2. j ___ l k ___ m n ___ p
3. v ___ x m ___ o d ___ f
4. e ___ g b ___ d p ___ r
5. g ___ i s ___ u h ___ j
6. q ___ s w ___ y c ___ e

Write the letter that comes before and after the given letter:

7. ___ c ___ ___ w ___ ___ s ___
8. ___ q ___ ___ e ___ ___ v ___
9. ___ h ___ ___ y ___ ___ t ___
10. ___ o ___ ___ k ___ ___ m ___

Alphabetical Order

Day 1

B Phonics

Name ___________________________

Write the words from each group in ABC order.

1. fire ______________
   ball ______________
   apple ______________
   circle ______________
   dime ______________
   earth ______________

2. heaven ______________
   Jupiter ______________
   God ______________
   light ______________
   keep ______________
   ice ______________

3. quarter ______________
   Orion ______________
   night ______________
   moon ______________
   planets ______________
   round ______________

4. want ______________
   stars ______________
   zenith ______________
   Venus ______________
   universe ______________
   telescope ______________

A Poetry Connection

Name ______________________

Slanted and Straight

The roof of our house slants this way and that,
It sits up on top like a party hat.

The walls of our house are tall and straight,
They're built very strong to hold up the weight.

The floor of our house is level and flat,
So things will stay put — I'm thankful for that!

Say the name of each picture.
Write the letter for the beginning sound to complete each name.

1. ____ed
2. ____oys
3. ____ink
4. ____icture
5. ____able
6. ____amp
7. ____esk
8. ____ug
9. ____indow

Beginning Consonants

Day 2

B Phonics

Name ______________________________

Say the name of each picture.
Circle the letter that stands for the beginning sound.

1. 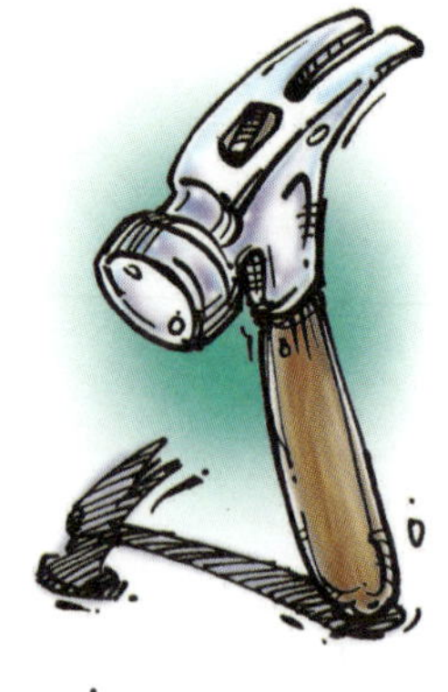

r h n m

2. 

b w d l

3. 

z s c w

4. 

m p b l

5. 

b p q k

6. 

w g r q

7. 

d p t z

8. 

f h g n

9. 

p r m n

A Poetry Connection

Name ______________________________

I wonder if . . .

Long ago and far away,
Children gathered 'round to play.
Swung a stick and hit a ball,
Lots of fun for one and all.

But the clay ball broke and cracked,
Every time that it got whacked!
So, making changes day by day,
They came up with other ways.

Today, we hear the baseball score,
Golf, softball, and many more.
Perhaps it started (could be true),
With children playing, just like you!

Say the name of each picture.
Write the letter for the beginning sound to complete each name.

1. 

___all

2. 

___ie

3. 

___oll

4. 

___og

5. 

___ame

6. 

___oat

B Phonics

Name ______________________

Say the name of each picture.
Write the uppercase and lowercase partner letters for the beginning sound.

Beginning Consonants

Day 3

1. 

____

2. 

____

3. 

____

4. 

____

5. 

____

6. 

____

7. 

____

8. 

____

9. 

____

A Poetry Connection

Name ______________________

Baby Toes

When I was a baby, small as could be,
Mom counted my fingers and toes.
She made up a song, to sing just for me,
And this is the way it goes . . .

One, two, — three, four, five . . .
Little bees buzzing out of the hive,
Five, four, — three, two, one . . .
Better look out, 'cause here they come!

Say the name of each picture.
Write the letter for the ending sound to complete each name.

Ending Consonants
Day 4

1. 

sta____

2. 

mitte____

3. 

win____

4. 

fou____

5. 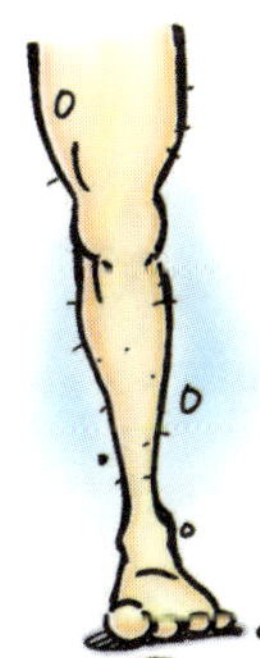

le____

6. 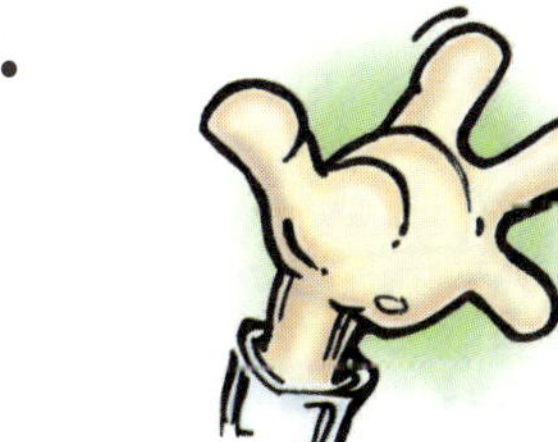

han____

B Phonics

Name ____________________

Say the name of each picture.
Write the letter for the ending sound.

1. 

______

2. 

______

3. 

______

4. 

______

5. 

______

6. 

______

7. 

______

8. 

______

9. 

______

A Poetry Connection

Name ______________________________

Growing Pains

When I was just six, age seven looked fine.
When seven, I longed to be eight!
And now that I'm eight, I just want to be nine,
For I know being nine would be great.

When I get to ten, I'll almost be grown!
But Dad says when I'm a man,
I'll wish for the day when I was a boy,
So be glad for the age that I am!

Say the name of each picture.
Find the picture whose name will best complete each sentence.
Write the missing letter to complete each name.

1. She had six le___ons for the pie.
2. That ti___er is big!
3. I ate se___en nuts.
4. The ca___el is brown.
5. Pull the red wa___on.
6. Did you see eight legs on the spi___er?
7. We can go to the ca___in.
8. This is my ra___io.

Medial Consonants

Day 5

Medial Consonants

Day 5

B Phonics

Name ______________________

Say the name of each picture.
Write the letter for the consonant sound you hear in the middle of each word.

1.  ______

2.  ______

3.  ______

4.  ______

5.  ______

6.  ______

7.  ______

8.  ______

9.  ______

A Poetry Connection

Name ______________________________

Otters at Play

Alphie and Danny were otter "best friends,"
That lived by a lake in the woods.
At the top of a mountain that everyone called,
"I'd-Climb-To-The-Top-If-I-Could."

Now, Alphie and Danny often played chase,
And wrestled and tickled and hid.
One day they were rolling and having such fun,
Straight down to the bottom they slid!

They couldn't climb up to get back to their home,
Going that way would take until dawn!
Then, they spotted a limber pine growing near by,
Bent it down, held it fast, and climbed on.

"Here we go," Danny cried, with a lopsided grin,
Alphie laughed, "We'll sure land with a plop!"
And when they let go . . . well, that tall, taut tree,
Sailed them up and right back to the top!

Say the name of each picture, and write the name on the first line. On the next line, write a word that rhymes with it.

1. ____________
2. ____________

5. ____________
6. ____________

3. ____________
4. ____________

7. ____________
8. ____________

The Sound of /o/

Day 6

B Phonics

Name ____________________

Circle the word that names each picture.

1. 

hot pot fox

2. 

doll otter top

3. 

box log rock

4. 

cob cot fox

5. 

pot lot rob

6. 

mob mop top

7.  

log just jog

8. 

tip pot top

9. 

dog hog done

A Poetry Connection

Name ______________________________

Deeds of Kindness

Every act of kindness,
Every word and deed,
Plants within someone's heart,
A tiny, happy seed.

The seed begins to blossom,
To send down roots and grow.
Soon happiness is passed along,
To everyone you know.

Circle the word that best completes each sentence and write it on the line:

1. Jen shared her blue ________.
   red pen best

2. Ted will ride on the green ________.
   sled bed desk

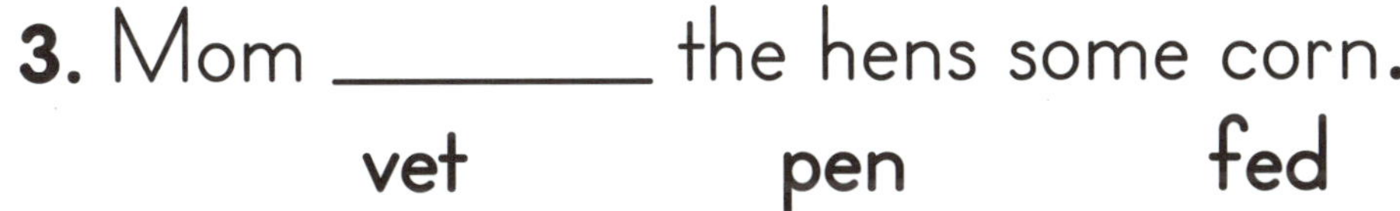

3. Mom ________ the hens some corn.
   vet pen fed

4. We gave the ________ flowers to Grandma.
   red bet peg

5. The ________ was the right size for Ben.
   get held tent

6. Tell Tom to ________ Dad.
   peck led help

7. I sat at a friend's ________.
   nest desk rest

B Phonics

Name ______________________________

Circle the word that names each picture.

1. 

hen hand pen

2. 

fed met nest

3. 

net web bed

4. 

peck sled vet

5. 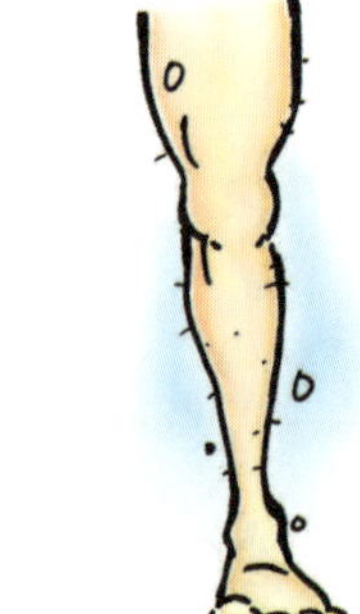

log leg lid

6. 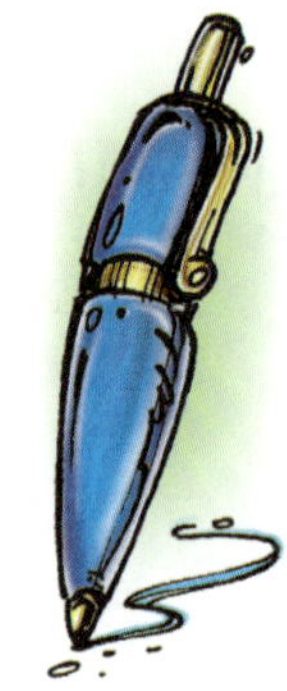

pan pen pond

7. 

belt bend bell

8. 

bed west web

9. 

tent jet peg

A Poetry Connection

Name ______________________________

Lots of Little Things

I always keep my pockets full,
With lots of little things,
Like marbles, pennies, bottle caps,
And tiny bits of string.

Sometimes, when Mama does the wash,
And dumps my pockets out,
I race into the laundry room,
Because I hear a shout!

There stands Mama, white as a sheet,
Trying not to cry.
'Cause Mama gets excited,
When my pocket stuff's ALIVE!

Color the oval in front of the sentence that tells about each picture.
Draw a circle around all **/i/** words.

1. ⬭ Bill bit his lip.
   ⬭ Bill will run up the hill.
   ⬭ Bill has an ink pen.
   ⬭ Bill drinks a lot of milk.

2. ⬭ Sid did spill the pins.
   ⬭ Sid will lift the lid.
   ⬭ Sid will eat the chips and dip.
   ⬭ Sid can fill the dish with dill.

3. ⬭ The king has a big pig.
   ⬭ The king put a dish in the sink.
   ⬭ The king hid in the big box.
   ⬭ The king sat on the big fish.

B **Phonics**

Name ______________________

Write the word that names each picture by filling in the missing letters.

1. 

___ i ___

2. 

___ i ___

3. 

___ i ___ ___

4. 

___ i ___ ___

5. 

___ i ___

6. 

___ i ___

7. 

___ i ___ ___

8. 

___ i ___

9. 

___ i ___ ___

A Poetry Connection

Name ______________________________

Truly Conceivable

Some say it's unbelievable,
And truly inconceivable,
Our Father made the birds that sing,
Long, long ago the stars did fling.

Some say it's unbelievable,
And truly inconceivable,
Our Father loves the world so much,
He sent His Son to die for us.

Some say it's unbelievable,
And truly inconceivable,
That Jesus wants to guide our way,
And care for us from day to day.

To me it's so believable,
And easily conceivable.
It's not because I'm really smart.
I know — because He's in my heart!

Say the name of each picture.
Circle the picture if the word has
the sound of **/u/** in the middle.

1. 

2.

3.

4.

5.

6.

B Phonics

Name ____________________

Circle the word that best completes each sentence and write it on the line.

1. I had a ________ of milk.
   cup bag

2. He saw a black ________ on the wall.
   bus bug

3. Russ can ________ and run.
   net jump

4. The dog sat on the ________.
   rug run

5. Did she ________ her leg?
   cut as

6. That white duck cannot ________ fast.
   cap run

7. I like red ________ the best.
   six gum

8. Was it ________ to ride the bike?
   fun kit

9. We sat in the hot ________.
   big sun

10. I gave my mom a big ________.
    hug hill

A Poetry Connection

Name ______________________________

Bubble Gum

I really do love chewing gum,
Blowing bubbles is lots of fun.
I chew gum quiet, chew it loud,
I chew alone, or in a crowd.

I chew it fast, I chew it slow,
But either way, one thing I know:
That when the flavor's gone at last,
I'll throw my gum into the trash.

For I know gum is fun to chew,
But not to find upon your shoe!
'Cause in my mouth it's soft and chewy,
But on the sidewalk, gross and gooey.

And so this promise I have made,
And with this promise I have stayed:
My chewing gum will not be found,
Upon the sidewalk, street, or ground!

Say the name of each picture.
Circle the picture if the word has the sound of **/g/**.

1. 

2. 

3. 

4. 

5. 

6. 

B Phonics

Name ______________________

Say each word. If it has the sound of **/j/**, write it in the top column. If the word has the sound of **/g/**, write it in the bottom column.

Soft g /j/

1. ______________________
2. ______________________
3. ______________________
4. ______________________
5. ______________________
6. ______________________
7. ______________________

Hard g /g/

8. ______________________
9. ______________________
10. ______________________
11. ______________________
12. ______________________
13. ______________________
14. ______________________

Word Bank

age	gave	giant	goes	goose	stage	wage
cage	gem	God	good	gym	tag	wagon

A Poetry Connection

Name ______________________

Mice in the Night

One night my mom went down the stairs,
And in the kitchen saw a pair,
Of mice behind the plastic bin,
She keeps the new potatoes in.

My mother gave a dreadful wail,
Then grabbed a bag and let it sail.
It flew — then landed with such fury,
That the mice began to scurry.

Then Dad ran into the kitchen,
He lost his balance, started slippin',
Because the floor was slick as ice —
My mom had thrown a bag of rice!

So now Dad has a broken arm,
Because of the "night mice" alarm.
If Mom ever sees more mice,
She'll grab a broom instead of rice!

Say the name of each picture.
Circle the picture if the word has the sound of **/k/**.

1. 

2. 

3. 

4. 

5. 

6. 

B Phonics Name ____________________

Circle the word that best completes each sentence and write it on the line.

1. The dog was __________ to me.
   nice face

2. Mike put the __________ in the bag.
   can race

3. Mom made a __________ cap for my doll.
   mice lace

4. I like __________ with milk.
   cement rice

5. You can bake a __________ for Dad.
   cake fence

6. This red __________ is too big for me.
   celery coat

7. Joe and Tom will run the __________.
   race rice

8. Please light the __________ on the cake.
   candies candles

9. Dad said not to climb the __________.
   fence fact

10. We went to see the __________.
    circus circles

Hard and Soft c

Day 11

A Poetry Connection

Name ______________________________

Compound Words

I've discovered, just like you,
That one plus one adds up to two.
But just today, I thought of this,
And realized a point I'd missed!

I had some oatmeal, creamy hot,
I sprinkled sugar on the top.
I watched that sugar melt right in,
I stirred it up, and thought with a grin . . .

There are some times when two together,
Add up to just one — one thing that's better!

Choose the two words that go best together to make a new word. You can make four new words from each set. Write the four new words on the lines.

tea	coat	1. ____________
sail	pot	2. ____________
mail	boat	3. ____________
rain	box	4. ____________
bath	boy	5. ____________
cow	road	6. ____________
rail	be	7. ____________
may	tub	8. ____________
base	mate	9. ____________
class	self	10. ____________
day	ball	11. ____________
my	dream	12. ____________

B Phonics

Name ____________________

Put each set of words together to make a new word. Write the word on the line then read the sentence.

1. oat+meal I like __________ with brown sugar.
2. pan+cake Mom puts butter on each __________.
3. cup+cake May I have a __________?
4. sea+weed There is __________ on the sand.
5. base+ball Will you play __________ next spring?
6. pea+nut We gave a __________ to the monkey.
7. rain+coat Did you wear a __________?
8. dog+house We helped Dad build a __________.
9. blue+berry Is this __________ ripe?
10. mail+box Take this letter to the __________.
11. foot+ball We like to play __________.
12. bath+tub Mom lets me wash in the __________.

Compound Words

Day 12

A Poetry Connection

Name ______________________

Right or Wrong

Right or wrong, right or wrong,
Sometimes its hard to know,
Whether something's right or wrong,
Or which way we should go.

But when we make bad choices,
And ask God to forgive,
He loves to take away our sins,
And show us how to live.

Name one of God's gifts to answer these riddles.
Each answer is a word with a final cluster.

1. I am an animal God made.
You do not like to have me around.
I am a __________.

2. Cows eat grass to make this.
I am something to drink.
I am __________.

3. Turtles and frogs live near me.
I am a good home for fish.
I am a __________.

4. Birds build this in a tree.
I am a home for their babies.
I am a __________.

Word Bank

milk   nest   pond   skunk

Final Clusters

Day 13

B Phonics

Name ___________________________

Say the name of each picture.
Write the final cluster to complete each word.

1. 

ri ___ ___

2. 

sta ___ ___

3. 

te ___ ___

4. 

sku ___ ___

5. 

mi ___ ___

6. 

ra ___ ___

7. 

ne ___ ___

8. 

li ___ ___

9. 

ce ___ ___

A Poetry Connection

Name ______________________________

Rainy Day

This morning's weather? We have rain!
I'm staring out the window pane,
And wondering what to do.

I guess that I could bake a cake,
Or make a purple play dough snake,
Or read a book or two.

I guess I could watch for the mail,
Or make a paper boat to sail,
Or build with sticks and glue.

But maybe, maybe if I wait,
The rain will start to dissipate,
And the sun will shine right through.

Then if Mother says, "Okay,"
I'll run right outside and play,
And find a friend or two.

Find the word that best completes each sentence and write it on the line.

1. Kate __________ a cake for Mom.
2. Steve can hike to the __________.
3. Dave put the __________ in the box.
4. We cannot __________ up late.
5. __________ the leaves into a pile.
6. Kay __________ the man for the grapes.
7. Put these roses in a __________.
8. What is his __________?

Word Bank

cave	mail	paid	stay
made	name	rake	vase

The Sound of /ā/, /ē/

Day 14

B Phonics

Name ______________________

Write the word that names each picture by filling in the missing vowels.

1. 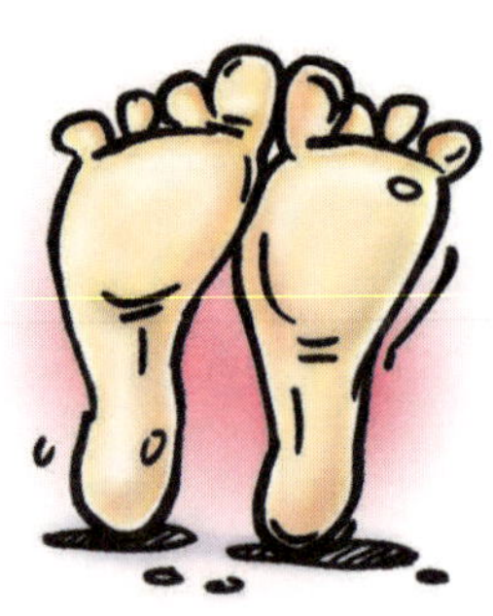

f ___ ___ t

2. 

j ___ ___ p

3. 

g ___ m ___

4. 

t ___ ___ th

5. 

tr ___ ___

6. 

r ___ ___ n

7. 

c ___ k ___

8. 

s ___ ___ l

9. 

sn ___ k ___

Word Bank

cake	game	rain	snake	tree
feet	jeep	sail	teeth	

A Poetry Connection

Name ______________________

My Perfect Day

The clouds are white and fluffy,
There's blue sky, there's sunshine,
The autumn leaves are colored bright,
The soft breeze feels just fine.

The pretty flowers are blooming,
Grapes ripen on the vine.
This day is simply perfect, Lord.
Thank you that it's mine.

Read each riddle and circle the correct answer.

1. It is something that blows gently. What is it?

   bread breeze

2. It can jump and hop. What is it?

   frog free

3. We sometimes eat it for a snack. What is it?

   grass fruit

4. This grows in the yard. What is it?

   train tree

5. It is something good to eat. What is it?

   grapes grade

6. It is something fun to play with. What is it?

   trail train

Clusters with r

Day 15

B Phonics

Name ______________________________

Circle the word that names each picture.

1. 

grapes grades

2. 

trust truck

3. 

from frog

4. 

drive drum

5. 

tree trim

6. train trade

Find the **r** cluster in each word and write the cluster letters on the line.

1. grapes ____________
2. truck ____________
3. train ____________
4. drink ____________
5. drum ____________
6. dress ____________
7. brick ____________
8. branch ____________
9. crowd ____________

A Poetry Connection

Name ______________________________

Faith in God

I look up to the heavens,
And think of God above.
I thank Him for His goodness,
His patience and His love.

I know that I can trust Him!
My faith in Him is strong.
He'll come again to take me,
Home, where I belong.

Read the sentence and circle the correct answer on the right. Circle the word or words in each sentence that has the sound of **/ü/** or **/ū/**.

Is it True?

1.	She can play a tune on a flute.	Yes	No
2.	The red shirt is blue.	Yes	No
3.	An ice cube is cold.	Yes	No
4.	A kitten is cute.	Yes	No
5.	Luke wrote part of the Bible.	Yes	No
6.	A mule eats at the table.	Yes	No
7.	I use a fork to write with.	Yes	No
8.	He can float on a tube.	Yes	No
9.	June is a day of the week.	Yes	No
10.	It is rude to hit others.	Yes	No

B Phonics

Name ______________________________

Circle words from the Word Bank as found in the puzzle.

r	p	L	e	b	c	f	t	u	b	e	f
u	c	u	b	e	g	i	k	m	l	o	q
d	a	k	e	s	r	t	v	J	u	n	e
e	x	e	z	a	c	c	u	t	e	g	e
h	m	j	l	m	o	p	s	r	t	u	w
t	u	n	e	b	d	f	e	a	r	v	y
f	l	u	t	e	u	j	u	y	h	i	f
e	e	s	b	o	r	u	l	e	t	h	a

Word Bank

blue	cute	June	mule	rule	tune
cube	flute	Luke	rude	tube	use

A Poetry Connection

Name ______________________________

Jesus is Kind

Mothers brought children for Jesus to bless,
But his helpers said, "No! He needs to rest."

The children turned sadly and started to go,
When Jesus said, "Come, I love children so!"

He kindly talked with them all through the day,
They were so glad He'd allowed them to stay.

Circle the **bold word** that best completes each sentence. Then, write it on the line.

1. Mark will hit the ball ________.
   high **hen** **hill**

2. She can ride her ________ today.
   bike **bill** **big**

3. I ________ to jump over the creek.
   lick **life** **like**

4. We made a ________ to get warm.
   five **fine** **fire**

5. There are a lot of bees in that ________.
   hit **hive** **hip**

6. Can you tell ________?
   tire **time** **tick**

7. The ________ under our sink broke.
   pipe **pit** **pie**

8. Jimmy has a big blue ________.
   kit **kite** **kick**

B Phonics

Name ______________________

Circle the word that best completes each sentence.

1. Will you jump (**rope, rod**) with me?
2. My dad needs to (**mop, mow**) the grass.
3. That (**got, goat**) is eating a shirt!
4. Mom wrote a (**not, note**) to my teacher.
5. Hang your (**coat, cot**) up on the hook.
6. There is a big (**hop, hole**) in this bag.
7. Tony (**rock, rode**) home with us.
8. My (**not, nose**) was cold and red.
9. Did you (**fog, fold**) the clothes?
10. The green (**toad, top**) croaked loudly.
11. The boys can (**row, romp**) the boat.
12. Ask (**Joan, jam**) to bring a robe.

A Poetry Connection

Name ______________________

Baby Bird

Follow me quick, but hush, now, hush,
There's something new in the blackberry bush.

A skinny thing, no feathers or fur,
It's cheeping and peeping, and causing a stir!

It wants food fast — but hush, don't speak,
Here comes Mama with a cricket in her beak.

Circle the **bold word** that best completes each sentence. Then, write it on the line.

1. The vase has a __________ at the top.
   crack **black**

2. I like to __________ in the tub.
   splash **dash**

3. Did you __________ your teeth?
   shine **brush**

4. A big __________ is at the dock.
   lock **ship**

5. His dog did a __________.
   trick **quack**

6. The pink __________ is on the sand.
   shell **snack**

7. He has black __________ on his feet.
   sacks **shoes**

8. I will clean the blue __________ with a cloth.
   stack **dish**

B Phonics

Name ______________________

Say the name of each picture. Circle the letters that stand for the consonant digraph in each name.

1. 

ck sh

2. 

sh ck

3. 

sh ck

4. 

sh ck

5. 

sh ck

6. 

sh ck

7. 

sh ck

8. 

sh ck

9. 

sh ck

A Poetry Connection

Name ______________________________

The Little Things

The puzzling thing about puzzles,
Is all the pieces you see.
When I first look at a pile of them,
They all look alike to me!

But I really try hard, and am happy to say,
That before I know it, I'm done.
Then feeling quite pleased, I think to myself,
"Now, I'll try a bigger one!"

Read each word. If the **y** has an **/ē/** sound, color that puzzle piece blue.

Underline each word in which **y** has an **/ī/** sound:

Tommy can fry an egg in this pan.

A plane can fly high in the sky.

There is a bunny by that tree.

Why did he cry when he saw the puppy?

B Phonics

Name ______________________

In each set, circle the word in which **y** has the sound of **/ē/**:

1.	**2.**	**3.**	**4.**
shiny	my	penny	tiny
fly	dry	try	fry
why	funny	shy	cry

Choose the word from the Word Bank below that best completes each sentence. Then write it on the line.

1. Please __________ to talk softly.

2. Put the ball __________ my books.

3. I have a dime to buy a piece of __________.

4. Billy can make __________ faces.

5. It is too __________ to fly my kite.

6. __________ are you crying?

Word Bank

by candy funny try why windy

A Poetry Connection

Name ______________________________

Hello, Mr. Wind

I love to hear the wild, wild wind,
Whipping and whistling through,
The open windows, under doors,
And up the chimney flue.

And though I know it's just the wind,
Doing what wind should do.
Sometimes it's funny to pretend,
It's someone I once knew.

So out I run to our front yard,
And wave my arms and yell,
"Hello there, friend! You going far?
You're rushing, I can tell!"

And as the leaves descend and swirl,
I pretend I hear him say,
"Just passin' through to say hello,
Can't stop to chat today!"

Read each riddle. Choose the correct answer and write it on the line.

1. I am a tool. A plumber uses me.
   What am I? ______________

2. I live in the ocean. I am very big.
   What am I? ______________

3. I grow in a field. I am used to make bread.
   What am I? ______________

4. I am part of a wagon. I am round.
   What am I? ______________

Word Bank

whale   wheat   wheel   wrench

B Phonics

Name ______________________

Circle the word that best completes each sentence and write it on the line.

1. ____________ out the wet towel.
   Wring   What

2. Brad fell and broke his ____________.
   wheat   wrist

3. Grandpa ____________ me a letter.
   wreck   wrote

4. ____________ are you going?
   Wren   Where

5. It is ____________ to tell a lie.
   wrong   whale

6. There are ____________ in her dress.
   wrinkles   write

7. Can you ____________ this gift?
   wheel   wrap

8. Did you eat the ____________ piece of cake?
   wrench   whole

9. We saw a ____________ on the "Ocean" video.
   wheat   whale

10. Dad is going to paint the house ____________.
    where   white

A Poetry Connection

Name ______________________

Six Little Eggs

Six little eggs in a mockingbird's nest,
Mother bird is warming them while she rests.

Father bird is singing the songs that he's heard,
And soon will be joined by six little birds!

Circle the word that best completes each sentence and write it on the line.

1. Timmy is outside __________ the dog.
   feed feeding feeds

2. Mr. Brown __________ on the fence all day.
   working works worked

3. Will you __________ to the store with me?
   walked walk walks

4. I like __________ down the creek in a tube.
   floated float floating

5. Our family went __________ at the lake.
   fishes fishing fished

6. Are you __________ for your mom?
   look looked looking

7. The frogs __________ into the pond.
   jump jumping jumped

8. Danny is __________ Allen with his math.
   helping helped helps

B **Phonics** **Name** ______________________________

Find the word that best completes each sentence and write it on the line.

1. We will be ______________ hot dogs at six.
2. Shelly is ______________ on one leg.
3. Bring your ______________ bag with you.
4. Which team is ______________ the game?
5. Adam is going ______________ at the pool.
6. They are ______________ candles to sell.
7. Mom took my sister ______________ for shoes.
8. Dad is ______________ at his job today.
9. The policeman is ______________ the cars.
10. I should buy a tent for our ______________ trip.
11. The children are ______________ for the bus.
12. Erin is ______________ the kitten.

Word Bank

camping	hopping	roasting	sleeping	swimming	winning
dipping	petting	shopping	stopping	waiting	working

A Poetry Connection

Name ______________________________

Hide and Seek

Our little brother likes to play,
The game of hide and seek.
But every time that he is "It,"
He always wants to peek.

So we explain, "You mustn't look,
Or you'll see where we run."
And every time, he nods his head,
And starts again at "one."

So off we go to find a spot —
That perfect hiding place.
But sure enough, we turn around,
To see that chubby face.

He'll laugh and squeal with sheer delight,
And grab us by the legs.
And though he just now caught us both,
"Play more!" he'll start to beg.

We roll our eyes and shake our heads,
Explain the rules again.
But I am thinking it would help,
If he could count to ten!

Say the name of each picture. Write the cluster that stands for the sound you hear at the beginning of each word.

1. 

____

3.  ____

5.  ____

2.  ____

4.  ____

6. 

____

Word Bank

bl cl dr fl pl st

Clusters with r, l, s

Day 22

B Phonics

Name ____________________

Find the word that best completes each sentence and write it on the line.

1. Dad can ________ stones on the lake.
2. We will ________ for the funny clown.
3. Put the cheese on that ________.
4. The dish is made of ________.
5. I like to pick ________.
6. Mike did not ________ the milk.
7. Did you ________ the can of peas?
8. The cake ________ very good.
9. Mr. Hanson drives a red ________.
10. A ________ is a black bird.
11. Mom wants us to use the rake on the ________.
12. My ________ are too small this winter.

Word Bank

clap	drink	glass	grass	skip	spill
crow	flowers	gloves	plate	smells	truck

A Poetry Connection

Name ______________________________

Character

School is fun, a happy place,
I'm learning lots of stuff!
But Mama says that learning math,
And spelling's not enough.

Our teachers here want us to know,
How children should behave.
So, when we first arrived at school,
These are the rules they gave:

"When walking down the hall, you must
March in single file."
"Hang up your coats on proper hooks,
Don't drop them in a pile."

"When time for lunch, your forks and spoons,
You really must not rattle."
"Be kind to all. Please understand,
It's very rude to tattle."

My mama says that this is good,
That "character" will grow.
And though I'm not sure what that means,
When I have it, it will show!

Find the word that best completes each sentence and write it on the line.

1. It is fun to __________ my sister.
2. Worms __________ in the mud after it rains.
3. The __________ of the pot is hot.
4. Dad put the __________ on the horse.
5. An __________ is a huge bird.
6. Do you like to eat __________?

Word Bank

eagle handle pickles saddle tickle wiggle

B Phonics

Name ____________________

Find the word that names each picture and write it on the line.

1. 

____

2. 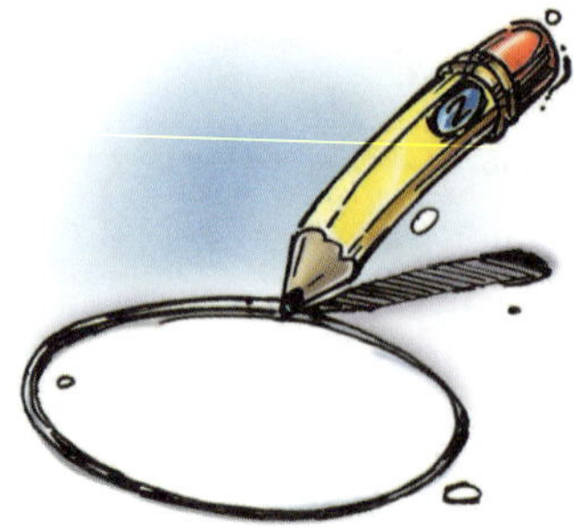

____

3. 

____

4. 

____

5. 

____

6. 

____

7. 

____

8. 

____

9. 

____

Word Bank

apple	buckle	circle	rattle	thimble
bubbles	candle	people	table	

Words Ending in -le

Day 23

A Poetry Connection

Name ______________________________

I've Been "Everywhere"

I've been to lots of places,
in the years I've been alive.
I've seen a million faces,
'cause my daddy likes to drive!

I've seen Ohio's rivers,
and Missouri's famous zoo.
I've been to Pennsylvania,
and covered Boston, too!

We stopped in Houston, Texas,
spent a day in Delaware.
Saw chickens in Rhode Island,
and toured the Kansas Fair.

Stood 'neath California's redwoods,
drove across Dakota's hills.
Stared amazed at Niagara Falls,
and Wisconsin's mighty mills.

Touched the Great Salt Lake in Utah,
then to Georgia made a trek.
Took my grandpa to Lake Erie,
after jaunting through Quebec.

When I say, we've been "everywhere!"
Dad spins the globe with glee.
His arms spread wide, as he declares,
"There's yet a world to see!"

Circle the word that best completes each sentence.

1. Her (**cheeks, peach**) are red from the cold.
2. (**Chin, Cheer**) for your favorite baseball team.
3. Dave sat in the blue (**chew, chair**).
4. (**The, They**) went to the park to play.
5. Please hand me (**that, those**) blocks.
6. (**Chop, Cheese**) wood for the fire, please.
7. Do you (**think, thing**) we can go?
8. I need to give my dog a (**thank, bath**).

B Phonics

Name ______________________

Say each word. If the consonant digraph is at the beginning of the word, write it in the first column. If it is in the middle, write it in the second column. If it is at the end, write it in the third column.

Beginning	Middle	End
1. ____________	6. ____________	11. ____________
2. ____________	7. ____________	12. ____________
3. ____________	8. ____________	13. ____________
4. ____________	9. ____________	14. ____________
5. ____________	10. ____________	

Word Bank

beaches	cheek	chips	coaching	peach	teacher	think
bench	chin	clothing	neither	reach	teeth	this

A Poetry Connection

Name ____________________

Jesus Loves Me

Jesus loves me! How do I know?
Things He created tell me so.

The pretty flowers in colors bright,
The moon and stars that shine at night.

The seasons as they come and go,
The rain and sun to help food grow.

God's Word with stories of long ago,
All tell of Jesus' love, I know.

Color in the oval in front of the sentence that tells about each picture. Draw a circle around each word that begins with the digraph **kn**.

1. ⬭ Jeff does not know the answer.
   ⬭ Jeff turned the door knob.
   ⬭ Jeff has a knot in his shoe lace.

2. ⬭ Nancy knelt down by her bed.
   ⬭ Nancy knocked on the door.
   ⬭ Nancy can knit a scarf.

3. ⬭ Dad put a new knob on the door.
   ⬭ Dad hit his knee on the chair.
   ⬭ Dad cut the bread with a knife.

Think of a word that starts with **kn** and rhymes with each word. Write it on the line.

1. snow ____________
2. hot ____________
3. see ____________
4. wife ____________
5. cob ____________

B Phonics

Name ______________________________

Circle the word that best completes each sentence and write it on the line.

1. Look at those shiny __________.
   star stars

2. We have many __________ in our yard.
   flower flowers

3. The __________ is very heavy.
   box boxes

4. We ate the bunch of __________.
   grape grapes

5. There are four __________ in a year.
   season seasons

Say each word. If the word means one, write it in the left column. If the word means more than one, write it in the right column.

One	More than One
1. ____________	6. ____________
2. ____________	7. ____________
3. ____________	8. ____________
4. ____________	9. ____________
5. ____________	10. ____________

Word Bank

apple	bowl	dishes	kitten	pencils
bananas	color	glasses	peaches	sandwich

A Poetry Connection

Name ______________________________

Matthew and Mark

I open my Bible, it's God's Holy Word.
I turn through the pages to stories I've heard.
I'm glad God had men write these stories so true,
So they'd be recorded for me and for you.

Matthew wrote about Jesus' birth,
His life and ministry while on earth.
Matthew proved Jesus is the Messiah,
Who fulfilled the prophecies of Isaiah.

Mark wrote of Jesus' ministry,
His life and teachings in Galilee.
Mark emphasized what Jesus did,
More than just what Jesus said.

Circle the word that names the picture.

1. 
can corn cone

2. 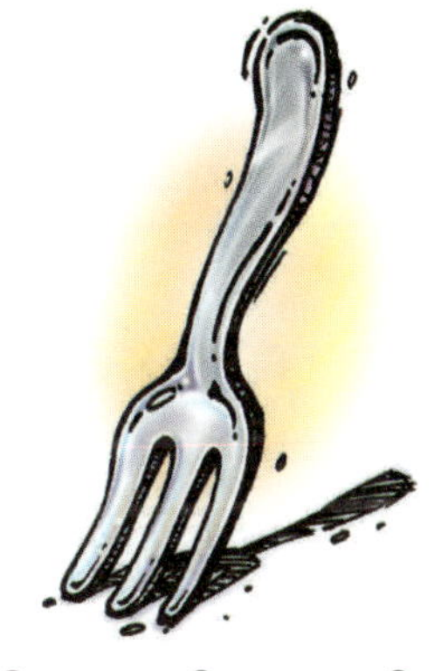
for fort fork

3. 
star stop stir

4.  
doll dart damp

5. 
barn back bark

6. 
have horse hope

B Phonics

Name ______________________

Read each riddle. To find the answer, think of a word that rhymes with the word at the end of each riddle. Write the answer on the line.

1. Pickles come in this.

   far ______________

2. You push this in a grocery store.

   mart ______________

3. A vegetable that grows on a stalk.

   born ______________

4. The opposite of light.

   bark ______________

5. Part of a car that makes a loud noise.

   torn ______________

6. It shines in the sky at night.

   bar ______________

7. A farmer keeps hay and tools in this.

   yarn ______________

8. A place to shop.

   more ______________

9. Something sharp on the stem of a rose.

   worn ______________

A Poetry Connection

Name ______________________

Luke and John

I open my Bible, it's God's Holy Word.
I turn through the pages to stories I've heard.
I'm glad God had men write these stories so true,
So they'd be recorded for me and for you.

Doctor Luke wrote his gospel in such a fine style,
Everyone understood it, both Jew and Gentile.
He wrote about Jesus from birth to ascension,
So we'd understand God's great salvation.

John speaks of Jesus in tones of such love,
That we look to the Father in Heaven above.
John tells us Jesus, who some called the Christ,
Brings truth, and salvation, and eternal life.

Circle the word that best completes each sentence.

1. Luke wrote about the __________ of Jesus.

   earth **birth** **burn**

2. I __________ the pages in my Bible carefully.

   verse **earn** **turn**

3. Jesus died so we can have __________ life.

   eternal **evening** **earnest**

4. It makes me happy to go to __________.

   crumb **church** **curb**

5. The __________ sang all morning.

   worms **birds** **chirp**

6. The little __________ is eating an acorn.

   squirrel **squash** **short**

Sound of /ûr/

Day 27

B Phonics

Name ______________________

Circle each word with the same sound as the name of the picture.

1.

bird / ir

first
shirt
horse
girl
thirty

2.

hurt / ur

fur
turtle
church
start
purse

3.

herd / er

germ
stern
short
merge
person

Find the name of each picture in the lists above. Write the names on the lines.

1.

____

2.

____

3.

____

A Poetry Connection

Name ______________________________

Fruits of the Spirit

Love helps boys and girls put their toys away.
Joy helps boys and girls be cheerful everyday.

Peace helps boys and girls be happy, never mad.
God's Spirit lives within their hearts,
And makes them very, very, glad!

Circle the word that names each picture.

1. 

tails toys tows

2. 

nose notes noise

3. 

point paint pint

4. 

boy boil bone

5. 

coins cons cones

6. 

say sail soil

7. 

boy done bone

8. 

all oil ail

9. 

coin cony coil

B Phonics

Name ______________________

Read each sentence. Find the word in the Word Bank that best completes each sentence. Write it on the line.

Diphthongs oi, oy

Day 28

1. The __________ won the race.
2. Some people collect stamps or __________.
3. The horn makes a loud __________.
4. __________ splatters are hard to clean.
5. A fruit of the spirit is __________.
6. He put __________ in the flower pot.
7. Sam got more __________ for his birthday.
8. The __________ on my pencil broke.
9. The water began to __________.
10. Would you like to __________ God's family?

Word Bank

boil	coins	joy	oil	soil
boy	join	noise	point	toys

A Poetry Connection

Name ______________________

House on the Rock

If you hear the words of Jesus,
But His voice you don't obey,
Then you are like that foolish man,
Who lost his house one day.

He had built upon the soft sand,
His foundations weren't dug deep.
When rain came down, and rivers flowed,
His house fell in a heap.

So please, put into practice,
All the words you hear God say.
He is the Rock, so you'll be strong.
Sin can't wash you away.

Read each riddle. Choose the correct answer and write it on the line.

1. I come in many colors.
   I grow in the yard. What am I? ______________
2. I am a direction.
   Birds fly this way in fall. What am I? ______________
3. I hunt at night.
   I live in a tree. What am I? ______________
4. I am something to wear.
   You'll wear one in heaven. What am I? ______________
5. A farmer uses me.
   I dig up the ground. What am I? ______________

Word Bank

crown flowers owl plow south

Diphthongs ou, ow

Day 29

B Phonics

Name ______________________

Read each sentence. Find the word in the Word Bank that best completes each sentence. Write it on the line.

1. There are pretty __________ in her yard.
2. A house built on sand will fall __________.
3. You must build your __________ on solid rock.
4. Jesus has promised us a __________ in heaven.
5. An __________ hooted near our tent.
6. Jesus will come in a __________ of angels.
7. Mother said I must go home __________.
8. The squirrel has __________ fur.
9. We went to __________ to do some shopping.
10. I learned __________ to plant a garden.

Word Bank

brown	crown	flowers	how	owl
cloud	down	house	now	town

A Poetry Connection

Name ____________________

Contradictions

The Pharisees and Scribes,
Who were teachers of the law,
Watched Jesus very closely,
Never liking what they saw.

They'd made a lot of extra rules,
For people to obey.
But Jesus showed the growing crowds,
That this is not His way.

God's laws were most important,
And not these rules of men.
Our Father loves and heals us,
And saves us from our sin.

Write the sentences in the correct order on the lines. Use a contraction in place of the underlined words. Remember to capitalize and punctuate correctly.

1. like Jesus. The Pharisees <u>did not</u>

____

2. obey God's laws. <u>I will</u>

____

3. happy help others. <u>We are</u> when we

____

4. <u>is not</u> My house built on sand.

____

Word Bank

didn't I'll isn't we're

B Phonics Name ____________________

Write the contraction that means the same as the words given.

Contractions: did not = didn't

1. did not ____________
2. cannot ____________
3. could not ____________
4. do not ____________
5. will not ____________
6. is not ____________
7. are not ____________
8. were not ____________

Contractions

Day **30**

Write the word or words that mean the same as the underlined contraction.

1. Jesus didn't worry about Pharisees. ____________
2. I won't tell the secret. ____________
3. Zacchaeus couldn't see over crowds. ____________
4. Peter isn't catching any fish. ____________
5. Why weren't you obeying Mom? ____________
6. The Pharisees don't want Jesus to heal on the Sabbath. ____________
7. They aren't coming with us? ____________
8. I can't wait until Jesus comes again. ____________

Word Bank

aren't	couldn't	don't	weren't
can't	didn't	isn't	won't

A Poetry Connection

Name ______________________

Sharing With Jesus

People loved Jesus, and Jesus loved them,
Wherever he went, crowds followed Him.
One day while preaching and healing the sick,
People kept coming, and crowds grew thick.

The disciples told Jesus, "The people can't stay,
We've nothing to feed them, they must go away."
But Jesus just asked them to wait for a while,
"My God will provide," He said with a smile.

"We do have some fishes and barley bread,
Offered up by a lad," Andrew said.
So Jesus took it, blessed it, and then,
It grew to feed five thousand men!

Enough for their families, for everyone there,
Because of a boy, who was willing to share.

Read each sentence. Write the correct suffix **-ed** or **-ing** on each line.

1. A boy want____ to hear Jesus' stories.
2. His mother is pack_____ him a lunch.
3. The people were listen_____ to Jesus.
4. Jesus ask____ if anyone had food.
5. The people were seat_____ on the grass.
6. Jesus asked a bless_____ on the food.
7. The disciples pass_____ out the food.
8. Jesus began break_____ the bread.

Suffixes -ed, -ing

Day **31**

B Phonics

Name ______________________

Read each riddle. Circle the base word in each underlined word. Answer each riddle, using words from the Word Bank.

Base Words: reading melted

1. I want to go listen to Jesus.
   My mother is packing me a lunch.
   Who am I? ______________

2. We were placed in a basket with some bread.
   There were two of us.
   What were we? ______________

3. We told the people to be seated.
   We were Jesus' special friends.
   Who were we? ______________.

4. I found a small boy with a lunch.
   I like talking to people.
   Who am I? ______________

5. I was put in a basket.
   Jesus blessed and broke me.
   What was I? ______________

Word Bank

Andrew bread disciples fish small boy

Remove this page and give to parent.

Dear Parent,

We are about to begin our first spelling unit containing five weekly lessons. A set of ten words plus three challenge words will be studied each week. All the words will be reviewed in the sixth week.

Values, based on each Scripture listed below, will be featured in that week's lesson.

Lesson 1	Lesson 2	Lesson 3	Lesson 4	Lesson 5
add	best	been	box	above
ask	ever	begin	dot	does
camp	head	digit	drop	done
fast	help	give	frog	jump
hat	left	into	gone	just
have	leg	its	lost	must
last	men	kid	lot	none
map	nest	live	odd	number
plan	next	quit	often	sum
than	set	sister	soft	what
☆ apple	☆ again	☆ because	☆ forgot	☆ bubble
☆ asked	☆ never	☆ gym	☆ job	☆ once
☆ bath	☆ sentence	☆ until	☆ tomorrow	☆ sometimes
Matt. 22:37	Luke 9:48	Matt. 5:25	Mark 9:50	Matt. 24:42

A Preview

Name ______________________

Write each word as your teacher says it.

1. ______________________

2. ______________________

3. ______________________

4. ______________________

5. ______________________

6. ______________________

7. ______________________

8. ______________________

9. ______________________

10. ______________________

Words with /a/

Lesson 1

Challenge Words

 ______________________

★ ______________________

★ ______________________

Scripture

Matthew 22:37

Words with /a/

Lesson 1

B Word Shapes

Name ____________________

Write each word in the correct Word Shape Boxes. Then, in the Word Shape Boxes, color the letter that spells the sound of **/a/** in each word. Circle words that begin with the sound of **/a/**.

1. add
2. ask
3. camp
4. fast
5. hat
6. have
7. last
8. map
9. plan
10. than

Challenge

Draw a Shape Box around each letter:

apple asked bath

C Hide and Seek

Name ___________________________

Circle a cookie for each word you spell correctly.

D Other Word Forms

Using the words below, follow the instructions given by your teacher.

adds	baths	has	maps
added	camps	had	mapped
adding	camped	hats	mapping
apples	camping	lasts	plans
asks	faster	lasted	planned
asking	fastest	lasting	planning

E Fun Ways to Spell

Initial the box of each activity you finish.

1. 

Spell your words with crayon . . .

3. 

Spell your words with rhythm instruments . . .

2. 

Spell your words with sidewalk chalk . . .

4. 

Spell your words with cotton balls . . .

Words with /a/

Lesson 1

F ABC Order

Name ______________________

Write each pair of spelling words in alphabetical order.

1. add hat ________ ________
2. plan camp ________ ________
3. map fast ________ ________
4. than ask ________ ________
5. have last ________ ________
★ bath apple ________ ________

TORNADO WARNING

VKJP TV

A B C D E F G H I J K L M N O P Q R S T U V W X Y Z

a b c d e f g h i j k l m n o p q r s t u v w x y z

G Dictation

Name ______________________

Listen and write the missing words.

1. Tommy _____ _____ _____ _____ _____.

2. _____ _____ _____ show _ _____ way.

3. Mrs. Morgan _____ _____ _____
___ _____ _____.

4. ___ like ___ hike better _____ _____.

H Proofreading

One word in each set is misspelled. Fill in the oval by the misspelled word.

1. ⬭ map ⬭ asc ⬭ hat

2. ⬭ hav ⬭ plan ⬭ than

3. ⬭ add ⬭ kamp ⬭ last

4. ⬭ fatst ⬭ ask ⬭ have

5. ⬭ than ⬭ map ⬭ plon

6. ⬭ lasd ⬭ camp ⬭ hat

★ ⬭ appel ⬭ fast ⬭ add

★ ⬭ plan ⬭ asket ⬭ add

★ ⬭ dath ⬭ last ⬭ have

I Game

Name ______________________

Follow Tommy to the pantry to sleep until the tornado is past. Move one space for each word you or your team spell correctly from this week's word list.

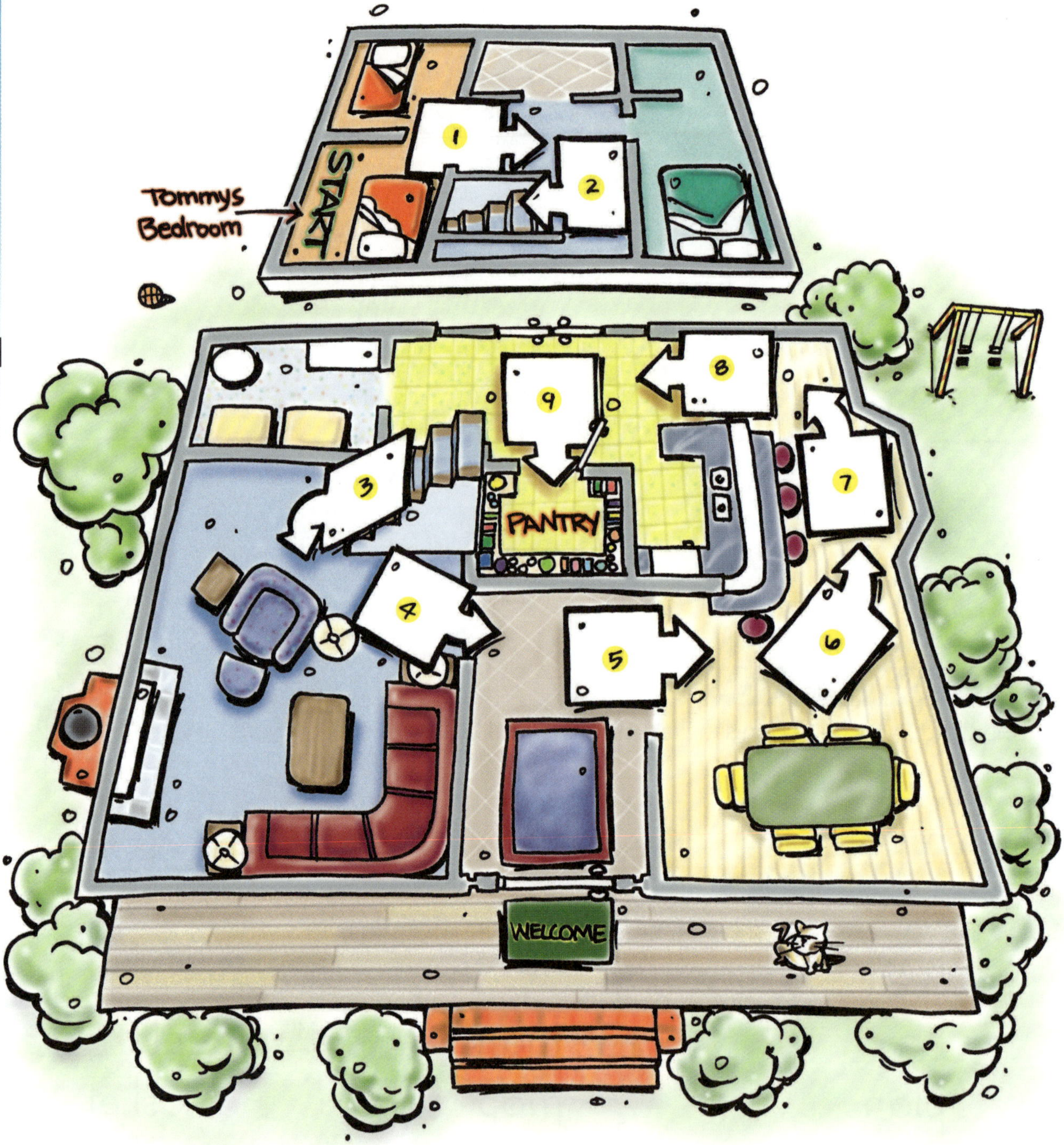

Remember: Choosing to be like Jesus shows that you love Him.

J Journaling

Copy this sentence and finish it:

I can show I love God with all my heart, soul, and mind by . . .

A Preview

Name ______________________

Write each word as your teacher says it.

1. ______________________

2. ______________________

3. ______________________

4. ______________________

5. ______________________

6. ______________________

7. ______________________

8. ______________________

9. ______________________

10. ______________________

Challenge Words

★ ______________________

★ ______________________

★ ______________________

Scripture

Luke 9:48

Words with /e/

Lesson 2

B Word Shapes

Name ______________________________

Write each word in the correct Word Shape Boxes. Then, in the Word Shape Boxes, color the letter or letters that spell the sound of **/e/** in each word. Circle the word in which the sound of **/e/** is spelled with two vowels.

1. best
2. ever
3. head
4. help
5. left
6. leg
7. men
8. nest
9. next
10. set

Challenge

Draw a Shape Box around each letter:

a g a i n   n e v e r   s e n t e n c e

C Hide and Seek

Name ______________________

Circle a cookie for each word you spell correctly.

D Other Word Forms

Using the words below, follow the instructions given by your teacher.

every	helps	legs	sentences
heads	helped	man	sets
headed	helping	nests	setting
heading	helper	nesting	reset

E Fun Ways to Spell

Initial the box of each activity you finish.

1. 

Spell your words with an eraser . . .

3. 

Spell your words with clapping . . .

2. 

Spell your words with paint . . .

4. 

Spell your words in damp sand . . .

F Letter Change

Name ______________________

Change the underlined letter or letters and write the spelling word on the blank.

1. ______________ Is there a baby bird in the neat?
2. ______________ Have you even seen a tornado?
3. ______________ The tornado loft a big mess.
4. ______________ The met put the trash in trucks.
5. ______________ Let those cups on the table.
6. ______________ The little boy was text in line.
7. ______________ He hid his hear behind his mom.
8. ______________ The dog's back log is in a cast.
9. ______________ I want to heap those in need.
10. ______________ Always do your very bust.

☆ ______________ I lever want to be in a tornado.

☆ ______________ They will build the houses train.

☆ ______________ This is the last sequence.

Word Bank

best	head	left	men	next	☆ again	☆ sentence
ever	help	leg	nest	set	☆ never	

G Dictation

Name ______________________

Listen and write the missing words.

1. ________ bird ________ ________

________ ________ I've ________ seen.

2. ________ ________ ________ ________

________ ________ door.

3. Daniel hurt ________ ________ ________

________ ________ ________ ________ ________ fell.

H Proofreading

One word in each set is misspelled. Fill in the oval by the misspelled word.

1. ◯ hed
   ◯ left
   ◯ nest

2. ◯ ask
   ◯ nexd
   ◯ camp

3. ◯ hat
   ◯ help
   ◯ mans

4. ◯ cet
   ◯ ever
   ◯ map

5. ◯ last
   ◯ lefd
   ◯ next

6. ◯ have
   ◯ set
   ◯ dest

★ ◯ agen
   ◯ apple
   ◯ bath

★ ◯ bath
   ◯ nevir
   ◯ asked

★ ◯ sintence
   ◯ apple
   ◯ asked

I Game

Name ______________________________

Tommy, Daniel, and James will carry the supplies for the families and pets of Center City into the warehouse. You lead the way by moving one space each time you or your team spell a word correctly from this week's word list.

Remember: Little things done for others shows our love for God.

J Journaling

Draw a picture in your journal of something you did to help someone else that made you feel great. Label your picture.

A Preview

Name ______________________

Write each word as your teacher says it.

1. ______________________

2. ______________________

3. ______________________

4. ______________________

5. ______________________

6. ______________________

7. ______________________

8. ______________________

9. ______________________

10. ______________________

Words with /i/

Lesson 3

Challenge Words

★ ______________________

★ ______________________

★ ______________________

Scripture

Matthew 5:25

B ## Word Shapes

Name ______________________________

Write each word in the correct Word Shape Boxes. Then, in the Word Shape Boxes, color the letter or letters that spell the sound of **/i/** in each word. Circle the word in which the sound of **/i/** is not spelled with an **i**.

1. been 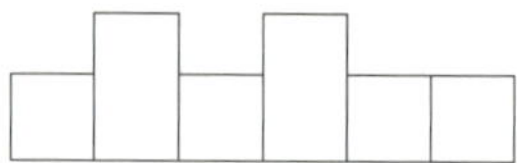
2. begin 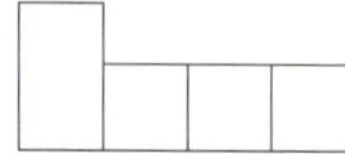
3. digit 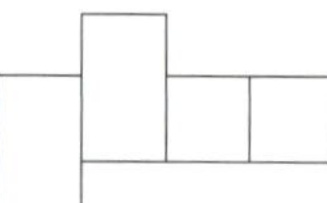
4. give 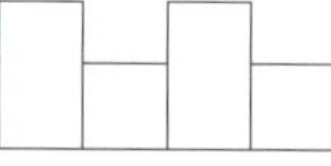
5. into 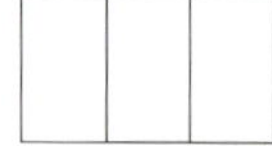
6. its 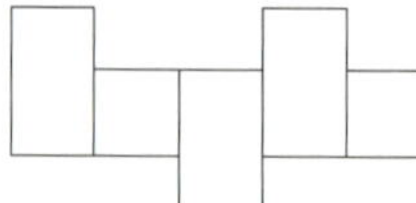
7. kid 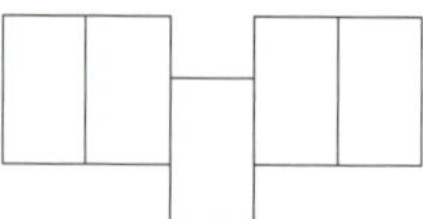
8. live 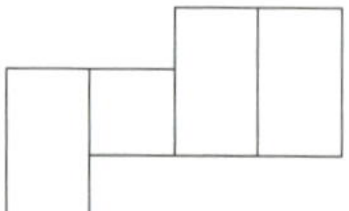
9. quit 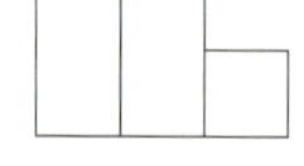
10. sister 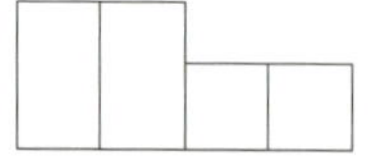

Challenge

Draw a Shape Box around each letter:

b e c a u s e   g y m   u n t i l

Words with /i/

Lesson 3

C Hide and Seek

Name ______________________________

Circle a cookie for each word you spell correctly.

D Other Word Forms

Using the words below, follow the instructions given by your teacher.

beginning	gyms	quits
begins	kids	quitter
digits	lived	quitting
gives	lives	sisters
giving	living	

E Fun Ways to Spell

Initial the box of each activity you finish.

1. 

Spell your words with puzzles . . .

2. 

Spell your words on a paper chain . . .

3. 

Spell your words out loud . . .

4. 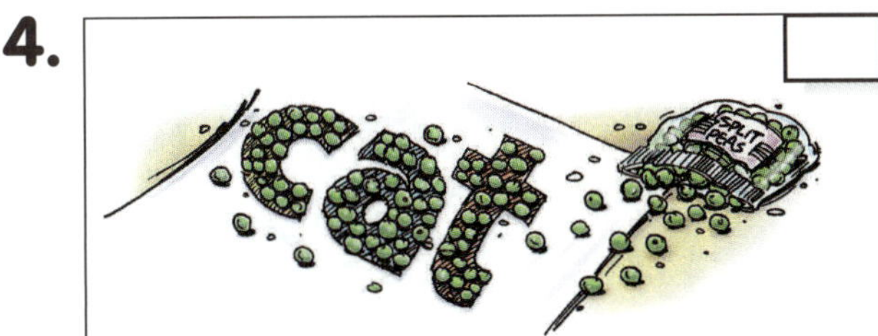

Spell your words with split peas . . .

Words with /i/ Lesson 3

Words with /i/

Lesson 3

F Word Change

Name ______________________

Write spelling words in place of the underlined word or words.

1. ______ The <u>number</u> you need to dial first is 9.
2. ______ Daniel is a nice <u>child</u> sometimes.
3. ______ Luke's <u>girl with the same parents</u> is Beth.
4. ______ Beth went <u>inside</u> the hospital to see Daniel.
5. ______ Have you <u>gone</u> to see Daniel?
6. ______ Daniel has a bandage and <u>the bandage's</u> color is white.
7. ______ The class will <u>hand over</u> a card to Daniel.
8. ______ <u>Stop</u> saying mean things to each other!
9. ______ Let's <u>start</u> by being kind to each other.
10. ______ <u>Dwell</u> in peace with each other.

★ ______ They weren't nice to each other <u>before</u> Daniel got hurt.

★ ______ Please glue this <u>since</u> it's broken.

★ ______ The class didn't go to the <u>play area</u> today.

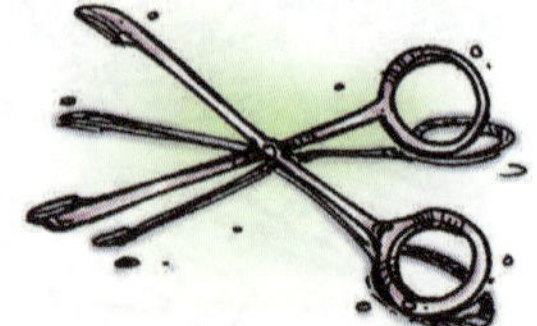

Word Bank

been	digit	into	kid	quit	★ because	★ until
begin	give	its	live	sister	★ gym	

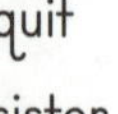
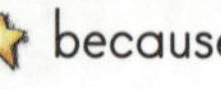

G Dictation

Name ___________________

Listen and write the missing words.

1. ________ calf ________ __________ calling

______ ______ __________.

2. ______ ________ _____ ________ piano

lessons soon.

3. Stephen ________ going ________

_________ room.

H Proofreading

One word in each set is misspelled. Fill in the oval by the misspelled word.

1. ◯ sistir
   ◯ give
   ◯ its

2. ◯ kid
   ◯ last
   ◯ beegin

3. ◯ men
   ◯ kwit
   ◯ best

4. ◯ deen
   ◯ live
   ◯ next

5. ◯ head
   ◯ intoo
   ◯ ever

6. ◯ dijit
   ◯ set
   ◯ help

★ ◯ jym
   ◯ never
   ◯ apple

★ ◯ sentence
   ◯ untill
   ◯ bath

★ ◯ again
   ◯ asked
   ◯ beecuz

I Game

Name ______________________________

Help Beth take a big bunch of balloons to Daniel at the hospital. Draw one string in Beth's hand (and place a balloon at the top) each time you or your team spell a word correctly from this week's word list.

Remember: Solve your problems with others quickly.

J Journaling

Draw a picture of some playground equipment you enjoy. Write two safety rules underneath the picture.

A Preview

Name ___________________________

Write each word as your teacher says it.

1. ___________________________

2. ___________________________

3. ___________________________

4. ___________________________

5. ___________________________

6. ___________________________

7. ___________________________

8. ___________________________

9. ___________________________

10. ___________________________

Challenge Words

★ ___________________________

★ ___________________________

★ ___________________________

Scripture

Mark 9:50

B Word Shapes

Name ____________________________

Write each word in the correct Word Shape Box. Then, in the Word Shape Boxes, color the letter that spells the sound of **/o/** or **/ô/** in each word. Circle words beginning with the sound of **/ô/**.

1. box
2. dot
3. drop
4. frog
5. gone
6. lost
7. lot
8. odd
9. often
10. soft

Challenge

Draw a Shape Box around each letter:

forgot job tomorrow

C Hide and Seek

Name ______________________

Circle a cookie for each word you spell correctly.

D Other Word Forms

Using the words below, follow the instructions given by your teacher.

boxes	dotting	lots
boxed	dropped	softer
boxing	dropping	softest
dots	frogs	softly
dotted	jobs	tomorrows

E Fun Ways to Spell

Initial the box of each activity you finish.

1.

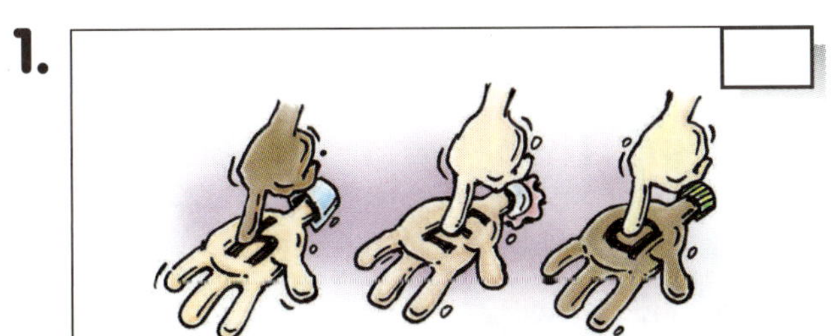

Spell your words in your classmate's hand . . .

3.

Spell your words out of the letter box . . .

2.

Spell your words with paper cups . . .

4.

Spell your words with shaving cream . . .

F Word Search

Name ______________________________

Using the Word Bank, Circle your spelling words in the puzzle. The words go across and down. Write each word in the correct blanks below.

t	o	m	o	r	r	o	w	z
b	o	f	r	o	g	b	l	o
o	g	l	d	f	t	d	o	d
x	o	f	o	r	g	o	t	d
e	d	d	t	x	o	f	l	x
w	r	g	x	f	n	t	o	s
s	o	f	t	p	e	e	s	o
x	p	t	t	o	r	n	t	r
d	o	i	j	o	b	d	o	w

Across

____

____

☆ ______________

☆ ______________

☆ ______________

Down

____

____

____

____

____

____

____

____

Word Bank

box	drop	gone	lot	often	 forgot	☆ tomorrow
dot	frog	lost	odd	soft	☆ job	

G Dictation

Name ______________________

Listen and write the missing words.

1. Kristin ______ ______ dime ______ ______ parking ______.

2. ______ ______ ______ ______ ______ catch ______ flies.

3. ______ clay ______ ______ ______ ______ very ______ color.

Words with /o/ or /ô/

Lesson 4

H Proofreading

One word in each set is misspelled. Fill in the oval by the misspelled word.

1. ◯ frog
◯ dot
◯ bocks

2. ◯ lost
◯ gon
◯ sister

3. ◯ od
◯ head
◯ lot

4. ◯ than
◯ quit
◯ ofen

5. ◯ best
◯ live
◯ sofd

6. ◯ leg
◯ brop
◯ map

★ ◯ because
◯ jod
◯ sentence

★ ◯ tomorow
◯ gym
◯ never

★ ◯ bath
◯ fergot
◯ again

I Game

Name ______________________

Place a game piece over each word your teacher says and spells. If the word appears on your card more than once, place a game piece over only one of the words. When you get five game pieces in a row, raise your hand and say, "Spelling is fun!"

Remember: When you do not feel like getting along with someone, you should choose to do it anyway.

J Journaling

Write a story about not feeling peaceful.
Draw a picture of the last time you were not at peace with someone.

A Preview

Name ______________________

Write each word as your teacher says it.

1. ______________________
2. ______________________
3. ______________________
4. ______________________
5. ______________________
6. ______________________
7. ______________________
8. ______________________
9. ______________________
10. ______________________

Challenge Words

☆ ______________________

☆ ______________________

☆ ______________________

Scripture

Matthew 24:42

B Word Shapes

Name ______________________________

Write each word in the correct Word Shape Box. Then, in the Word Shape Boxes, color the letter or letters that spell the sound of **/u/** in each word. Circle the words in which **/u/** is spelled with **a** or **o**.

1. above
2. does
3. done
4. jump
5. just
6. must
7. none
8. number
9. sum
10. what

Challenge

Draw a Shape Box around each letter:

b u b b l e   o n c e   s o m e t i m e s

C Hide and Seek

Name ____________________

Circle a cookie for each word you spell correctly.

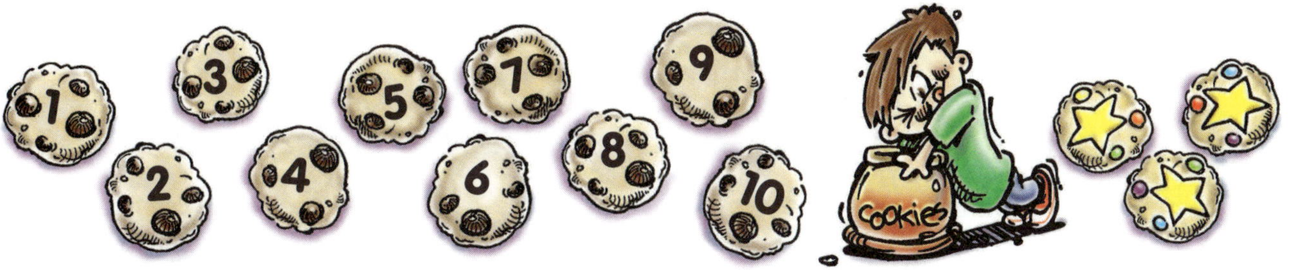

D Other Word Forms

Using the words below, follow the instructions given by your teacher.

bubbles	numbers	jumps	sums
bubbled	numbered	jumped	
bubbling	numbering	jumping	

E Fun Ways to Spell

Initial the box of each activity you finish.

1.

Spell your words with markers . . .

3.

Spell your words with snapping . . .

2.

Spell your words with letter tiles . . .

4.

Spell your words with finger paint . . .

F Sentence Order

Name ______________________________

Place each set of word groups in order to write a sentence. Circle the spelling words.

Jesus coming I must see  from above.

1. ______________________________

Coach Larkin  What does  ask Tony ?

2. ______________________________

up and  Just jump  hit the ball.

3. ______________________________

When you are done  the number.  write

4. ______________________________

of the sums  is correct.  None

5. ______________________________

we make  Sometimes  mistakes.

____

want a  Tony does not  bubble bath.

 ______________________________

may play  Tony  once he cleans up.

 ______________________________

Word Bank

above	done	just	none	sum	bubble	 sometimes
does	jump	must	number	what	once	

Words with /u/

Lesson 5

G Dictation

Name ______________________

Listen and write the missing words.

1. _____ _____ over this rope.

2. _____ _____ _____ first _____ _____

_____ _____?

3. Christopher _____ _____ _____ _____

_____ chores yet.

4. _____ _____ _____ __ find _____ _____.

H Proofreading

One word in each set is misspelled. Fill in the oval by the misspelled word.

1. ⬭ none
   ⬭ whot
   ⬭ jump

2. ⬭ duz
   ⬭ number
   ⬭ soft

3. ⬭ dun
   ⬭ number
   ⬭ just

4. ⬭ drop
   ⬭ nust
   ⬭ camp

5. ⬭ nest
   ⬭ abuv
   ⬭ set

6. ⬭ som
   ⬭ often
   ⬭ frog

★ ⬭ buble
   ⬭ tomorrow
   ⬭ until

★ ⬭ again
   ⬭ apple
   ⬭ sumtimes

★ ⬭ wunce
   ⬭ print
   ⬭ never

Words with /u/ Lesson 5

I Game

Name ____________________

Run a drill through the cones with Tony or Stephen. Color one space for each word you or your team spells correctly from this week's word list.

Remember: Live as though Jesus was coming today!

J Journaling

Write a story about how you can get to know Jesus.

A Test-Words

Name ______________________________

Write each spelling word on the line as your teacher says it.

1. ______________________ 6. ______________________

2. ______________________ 7. ______________________

3. ______________________ 8. ______________________

4. ______________________ 9. ______________________

5. ______________________ 10. ______________________

Review

Lesson 6

B Test-Sentences

The two underlined words in each of the sentences are misspelled. Write the sentences on the lines below, spelling each underlined word correctly.

Show Gawd's love by the way you liv.

1. ____

Jesus was gled Rosa had ben kind.

2. ____

It is tim to kwit.

3. ____

☆ Test-Challenge Words

Write each challenge word as your teacher says it.

Review

Lesson 6

C Test-Dictation

Name ______________________________

Listen and write the missing words.

1. ________ ______ piñata __________ __________?

2. __________ __________ _________ ______ ________

________ right ________.

3. ________ ________ candy ________ __________

______ ________ ground.

D Test-Proofreading

One word in each set is misspelled. Fill in the oval by the misspelled word.

1. ◯ kamp ◯ last ◯ above
2. ◯ been ◯ min ◯ next
3. ◯ just ◯ dijit ◯ soft
4. ◯ offen ◯ sister ◯ begin
5. ◯ plan ◯ have ◯ numbr
6. ◯ box ◯ gone ◯ od
7. ◯ dott ◯ drop ◯ lot
8. ◯ into ◯ kib ◯ live
9. ◯ done ◯ maq ◯ hat

☆ Test-Challenge Words

Write each challenge word as your teacher says it.

E Test-Shapes

Name ______________________________

Color each piece of candy on which the word is spelled incorrectly.

☆ Test-Challenge Words

Write each challenge word as your teacher says it.

Review
Lesson 6

Review

Lesson 6

F Game

Name ______________________________

Rosa showed Jesus' love when she unselfishly bought her brother and sister lollipops. The kind of lollipops they chose will be your team names for this game. Place a sticker each time you or your team spell a review word correctly.

Remember: Love others so they can see Jesus' love through you.

G Test-Words

Name ______________________

Write each spelling word on the line as your teacher says it.

1. ____________ 6. ____________

2. ____________ 7. ____________

3. ____________ 8. ____________

4. ____________ 9. ____________

5. ____________ 10. ____________

Review

Lesson 6

H Test-Sentences

The two underlined words in each of the sentences are misspelled. Write the sentences on the lines below, spelling each underlined word correctly.

Rosa got a nise craft cet.

1. ______________________________

Rosa's new reb shirt was very souft.

2. ______________________________

Which wun do you like the dest?

3. ______________________________

☆ Test-Challenge Words

Write each challenge word as your teacher says it.

I Writing Assessment

Name ______________________

Write a paragraph telling how everyone will be able to see that you are Jesus' disciple by your actions. Write at least four sentences.

____

____

____

____

____

____

____

Review

Lesson 6

Scripture

John 13:35

This certificate is awarded to:

____

for practicing the following words, doing terrific spelling activities and playing great spelling games!

Date ________________________

add	best	been	box	above
ask	ever	begin	dot	does
camp	head	digit	drop	done
fast	help	give	frog	jump
hat	left	into	gone	just
have	leg	its	lost	must
last	men	kid	lot	none
map	nest	live	odd	number
plan	next	quit	often	sum
than	set	sister	soft	what
★ apple	★ again	★ because	★ forgot	★ bubble
★ asked	★ never	★ gym	★ job	★ once
★ bath	★ sentence	★ until	★ tomorrow	★ sometimes

Dear Parent,

We are about to begin a new spelling unit containing five weekly lessons. A set of ten words plus three challenge words will be studied each week. All the words will be reviewed in the sixth week.

Values, based on each Scripture listed below, will be featured in that week's lesson.

Lesson 7	Lesson 8	Lesson 9	Lesson 10	Lesson 11
bake	be	buy	boat	blow
cake	clean	cry	cold	grow
came	east	dry	hold	know
game	even	fly	home	low
gate	he's	I'm	hope	own
gave	keep	light	most	row
grade	people	might	old	slow
late	read	night	road	snow
name	tree	right	roll	throw
page	we'll	tie	told	tow
☆ break	☆ between	☆ Bible	☆ don't	☆ below
☆ great	☆ Jesus	☆ child	☆ over	☆ mowing
☆ obey	☆ sleep	☆ high	☆ wrote	☆ snowman
Mark 5:19	Luke 11:36	Luke 1:46, 47	Matthew 22:39	Luke 21:33

A Preview

Name ______________________

Write each word as your teacher says it.

1. ______________________

2. ______________________

3. ______________________

4. ______________________

5. ______________________

6. ______________________

7. ______________________

8. ______________________

9. ______________________

10. ______________________

Challenge Words

★ ______________________

★ ______________________

★ ______________________

Scripture

Mark 5:19

B Word Shapes

Name ______________________

Write each word in the correct Word Shape Box. Then, in the Word Shape Boxes, color the letters that spell the sound of **/ā/** in each word. Circle the word that begins with the consonant cluster **gr**.

1. bake
2. cake
3. came
4. game
5. gate
6. gave
7. grade
8. late
9. name
10. page

Challenge

Draw a Shape Box around each letter:

b r e a k   g r e a t   o b e y

C Hide and Seek

Name ____________________

Circle a cookie for each word you spell correctly.

D Other Word Forms

Using the words below, follow the instructions given by your teacher.

bakes	caked	graded	latest	pages
baked	games	grading	names	
baking	gates	grader	named	
cakes	grades	later	naming	

E Fun Ways to Spell

Initial the box of each activity you finish.

1. ☐

Spell your words with crayon . . .

2. ☐

Spell your words with sidewalk chalk . . .

3. ☐

Spell your words with rhythm instruments . . .

4. ☐

Spell your words with cotton balls . . .

Words with /ā/

Lesson 7

F ABC Order

Name ______________________

Write each set of spelling words in alphabetical order.

1. gate ____________
   late ____________
   grade ____________

2. came ____________
   bake ____________
   cake ____________

3. game ____________
   name ____________
   page ____________

4. gave ____________
   came ____________
   grade ____________

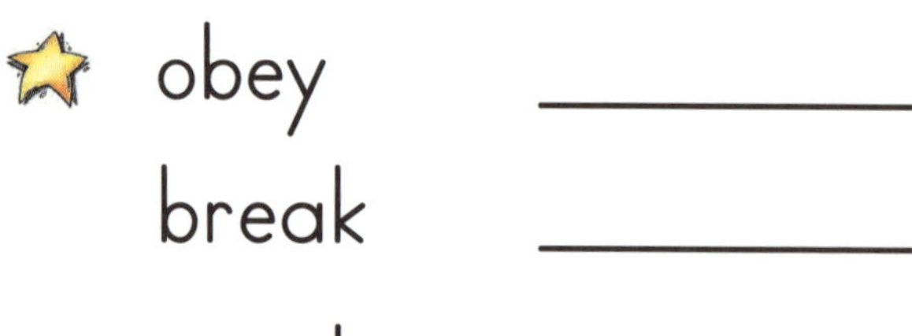

★ obey ____________
   break ____________
   great ____________

A B C D E F G H I J K L M N O P Q R S T U V W X Y Z

a b c d e f g h i j k l m n o p q r s t u v w x y z

G Dictation

Name ___________________________

Listen and write the missing words.

1. Setsuko ________ ________ ______ ________.

2. ______ ______ leaped over ______ ______.

3. Katelynn wrote ________ ________

________ ________ ________ ________.

4. __________ teacher __________ each

student ________ ________.

H Proofreading

One word in each set is misspelled. Fill in the oval by the misspelled word.

1. ◯ gate
   ◯ paje
   ◯ digit

2. ◯ kame
   ◯ gave
   ◯ its

3. ◯ gane
   ◯ kid
   ◯ grade

4. ◯ give
   ◯ name
   ◯ laete

5. ◯ add
   ◯ dake
   ◯ odd

6. ◯ kake
   ◯ been
   ◯ late

★ ◯ obay
  ◯ gym
  ◯ bubble

★ ◯ forgot
  ◯ sometimes
  ◯ brack

★ ◯ grat
  ◯ because
  ◯ job

Words with /ā/

Lesson 7

Words with /ā/

Lesson 7

I Game

Name ______________________

Get in line to ride the Firebird Roller Coaster. Move up in line one space for each word you or your team spell correctly from this week's word list.

FANTASTIC FUN FAIR

start

the Firebird

Remember: Praise God for each special thing He does for you!

J Journaling

Write three sentences about wonderful things God has done for you.

A Preview

Name ______________________

Write each word as your teacher says it.

1. ______________________

2. ______________________

3. ______________________

4. ______________________

5. ______________________

6. ______________________

7. ______________________

8. ______________________

9. ______________________

10. ______________________

Words with /ē/

Lesson 8

Challenge Words

★ ______________________

★ ______________________

★ ______________________

Scripture

Luke 11:36

B Word Shapes

Name ______________________

Write each word in the correct Word Shape Boxes. Then, in the Word Shape Boxes, color the letter or letters that spell the sound of **/ē/** in each word. Circle the words that are contractions. Draw a line under the words that begin with the consonant clusters **cl** or **tr**.

1. be
2. clean
3. east
4. even
5. he's
6. keep
7. people
8. read
9. tree
10. we'll

Challenge

Draw a Shape Box around each letter:

between Jesus sleep

Words with /ē/

Lesson 8

C Hide and Seek

Name ______________________________

Circle a cookie for each word you spell correctly.

D Other Word Forms

Using the words below, follow the instructions given by your teacher.

been	cleanest	keeps	reader
cleans	unclean	kept	sleeps
cleaned	eastern	keeping	slept
cleaning	evening	reads	sleeping
cleaner	uneven	reading	trees

E Fun Ways to Spell

Initial the box of each activity you finish.

1. 

Spell your words with an eraser . . .

2. 

Spell your words with paint . . .

3. 

Spell your words with clapping . . .

4. 

Spell your words in damp sand . . .

F Clues

Name ______________________

Use the clues to write the spelling words.

1. __________ he is
2. __________ we will
3. __________ not odd
4. __________ not dirty
5. __________ human beings
6. __________ fulfill, like a promise
7. __________ exist or to take place
8. __________ a tall plant with a trunk
9. __________ face this way to see the sun rise
10. __________ know what written words mean

☆ __________ in the middle of

☆ __________ to take a nap

☆ __________ the Son of God

Word Bank

be, clean, east, even, he's, keep, people, read, tree, we'll, ☆ between, ☆ Jesus, ☆ sleep

G Dictation

Name ______________________

Listen and write the missing words.

1. ________ ________ like ______ ________

______ newspaper.

2. ________ ________ ________ ________ towels

______ here.

3. ________ climbing ____ ________ ________.

4. ________ sure ________ feed ______ ______.

H Proofreading

One word in each set is misspelled. Fill in the oval by the misspelled word.

1. ⬭ bake
   ⬭ cleen
   ⬭ we'll

2. ⬭ live
   ⬭ soft
   ⬭ de

3. ⬭ done
   ⬭ leg
   ⬭ peepl

4. ⬭ reab
   ⬭ even
   ⬭ tree

5. ⬭ late
   ⬭ eest
   ⬭ he's

6. ⬭ keap
   ⬭ set
   ⬭ head

★ ⬭ job
   ⬭ betwean
   ⬭ once

★ ⬭ jesus
   ⬭ obey
   ⬭ because

★ ⬭ forgot
   ⬭ never
   ⬭ sleap

I Game

Name ______________________________

Retrace Christopher's path the day he broke his arm. Move one space each time you or your team spell a word correctly from this week's word list.

Remember: Let your face reflect that Jesus lives in your heart!

J Journaling

Write a prayer asking God to fill you with His love.

A Preview

Name ______________________

Write each word as your teacher says it.

1. ______________________

2. ______________________

3. ______________________

4. ______________________

5. ______________________

6. ______________________

7. ______________________

8. ______________________

9. ______________________

10. ______________________

Challenge Words

★ ______________________

★ ______________________

★ ______________________

Scripture

Luke 1:46, 47

B Word Shapes

Name ______________________________

Write each word in the correct Word Shape Boxes. Then, in the Word Shape Boxes, color the letter or letters that spell the sound of /ī/ in each word. Circle the word that has a contraction. Draw a line under the silent letters **gh**.

1. buy
2. cry
3. dry
4. fly
5. I'm
6. light
7. might
8. night
9. right
10. tie

Challenge

Draw a Shape Box around each letter:

Bible   child   high

Words with /ī/

Lesson 9

C Hide and Seek

Name ______________________________

Circle a cookie for each word you spell correctly.

D Other Word Forms

Using the words below, follow the instructions given by your teacher.

Bibles	crying	higher	lightest	ties
buys	dries	highest	mighty	tied
bought	dried	I	mightier	tying
buying	drying	lights	mightiest	
children	flies	lighted	nights	
cries	flew	lighting	nightly	
cried	flying	lighter	rights	

E Fun Ways to Spell

Initial the box of each activity you finish.

1. 

Spell your words with puzzles . . .

2. 

Spell your words on a paper chain . . .

3. 

Spell your words out loud . . .

4. 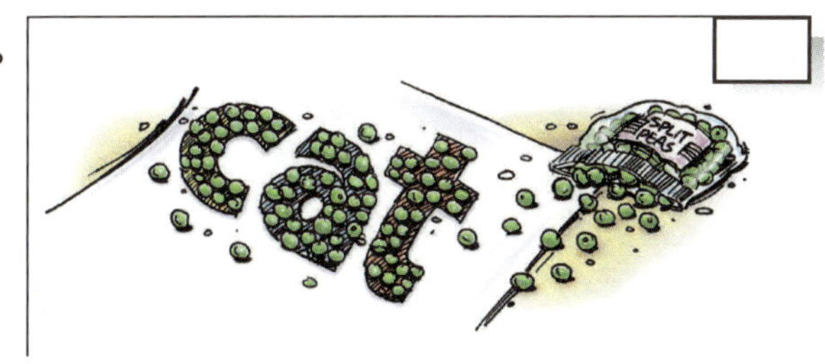

Spell your words with split peas . . .

Words with /ī/

Lesson 9

Words with /ī/

Lesson 9

F Words in Sentences

Name ______________________

Use the picture key to find the word in the Word Bank that best completes each sentence. Write it in the blank.

1. It ________ start to rain soon.

2. Turn the playroom ________ on.

3. Always make the ________ choice.

4. It may rain all ________.

5. You ________ when you feel sad.

6. This ball can really ________.

7. You need to ________ your shoe.

8. The umbrella keeps you ________.

9. They will ________ a new screen.

10. ________ glad God saves me!

Word Bank

 dry, might

 night

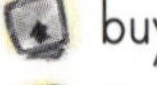 buy, fly

 light, tie

 cry, I'm

 right

G Dictation

Name ______________________

Listen and write the missing words.

1. _____ going _____ _____ _____ dishes.

2. _____ _________ _______ my kite today.

3. _____ street _______ comes _____

_______ _________.

4. Rosa wants _____ _______ _____ doll

________ _______ _______.

H Proofreading

One word in each set is misspelled. Fill in the oval by the misspelled word.

1. ⬭ nest
   ⬭ kry
   ⬭ I'm

2. ⬭ nite
   ⬭ gave
   ⬭ gone

3. ⬭ fly
   ⬭ tye
   ⬭ live

4. ⬭ duy
   ⬭ right
   ⬭ than

5. ⬭ migt
   ⬭ begin
   ⬭ sum

6. ⬭ bry
   ⬭ light
   ⬭ left

☆ ⬭ apple
   ⬭ chid
   ⬭ great

☆ ⬭ gym
   ⬭ bible
   ⬭ sentence

☆ ⬭ break
   ⬭ tomorrow
   ⬭ hy

I Game

Name ______________________________

Daniel and Tommy made a poor choice to throw the ball inside the house. Follow the path of the baseball toward the computer screen. Color one space for each word you or your team spell correctly from this week's word list.

Start

Remember: God always loves us and wants to forgive us.

J Journaling

Write four or more sentences about a time when you were in trouble and needed help.

A Preview

Name ______________________________

Write each word as your teacher says it.

1. ______________________
2. ______________________
3. ______________________
4. ______________________
5. ______________________
6. ______________________
7. ______________________
8. ______________________
9. ______________________
10. ______________________

Challenge Words

☆ ______________________

☆ ______________________

☆ ______________________

Scripture

Matthew 22:39

Words with /ō/

Lesson 10

B Word Shapes

Name ______________________________

Write each word in the correct Word Shape Boxes. Then, in the Word Shape Boxes, color the letter or letters that spell the sound of **/ō/** in each word. Circle the words in which **/ō/** is spelled with **o-e**. Draw a line under the words in which **/ō/** is spelled with **oa**.

1. boat
2. cold
3. hold
4. home
5. hope
6. most
7. old
8. road
9. roll
10. told

Challenge

Draw a Shape Box around each letter:

d o n ' t   o v e r   w r o t e

C Hide and Seek

Name ___________________________

Circle a cookie for each word you spell correctly.

D Other Word Forms

Using the words below, follow the instructions given by your teacher.

boats	held	hoping	oldest	rolling
boating	holding	hopeful	overly	roller
colder	homes	hopeless	roads	tell
coldest	hopes	mostly	rolls	tells
holds	hoped	older	rolled	telling

E Fun Ways to Spell

Initial the box of each activity you finish.

1. 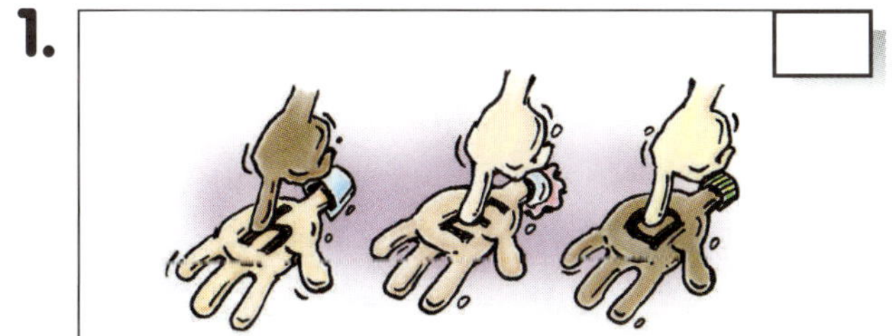

Spell your words in your classmate's hand . . .

3. 

Spell your words out of the letter box . . .

2. 

Spell your words with paper cups . . .

4. 

Spell your words with shaving cream . . .

F Crossword

Name ______________________________

Use the puzzle clues to write the spelling words.

Across

1. Not hot
2. I tell today, I _______ yesterday.
4. more than anything else
6. place where you live
8. to grab something and not let go

Down

3. This is a yummy sweet _______.
5. We drive down the _______.
7. travels on water
8. a feeling that things will get better
9. not young

Word Bank

boat	hold	hope	old	roll
cold	home	most	road	told

Words with /ō/

Lesson 10

G Dictation

Name ______________________

Listen and write the missing words.

1. ______ ______ ______ ______ bumpy.

2. Tony ______ ______ ______ ______ ______ carefully.

3. ______ enjoyed ______ ______ ______ ______ ______.

4. ______ ______ ______ water ______ ______ ______.

Words with /ō/

Lesson 10

H Proofreading

One word in each set is misspelled. Fill in the oval by the misspelled word.

1. ○ bote
   ○ most
   ○ hat

2. ○ fast
   ○ hoam
   ○ road

3. ○ best
   ○ tree
   ○ haop

4. ○ dot
   ○ must
   ○ odl

5. ○ next
   ○ rol
   ○ light

6. ○ kold
   ○ hold
   ○ told

★ ○ ovr
   ○ bath
   ○ sometimes

★ ○ until
   ○ never
   ○ bon't

★ ○ again
   ○ asked
   ○ roet

I Game

Name ______________________________

Place a game piece over each word your teacher says and spells. If the word appears on your card more than once, place a game piece over only one of the words each time it is said. When you get five game pieces in a row, raise your hand and say, "Spelling is fun!"

		FREE		

Remember: Do kind things for others as you would do them for yourself.

J Journaling

Make a list of ways your actions can show you love your neighbor as you love yourself.

A Preview

Name ____________________

Write each word as your teacher says it.

1. ____________________

2. ____________________

3. ____________________

4. ____________________

5. ____________________

6. ____________________

7. ____________________

8. ____________________

9. ____________________

10. ____________________

Words with /ō/

Lesson 11

Challenge Words

★ ____________________

★ ____________________

★ ____________________

Scripture

Luke 21:33

B Word Shapes

Name ______________________

Write each word in the correct Word Shape Box. Then, in the Word Shape Boxes, color the letters that spell the sound of /ō/ in each word. Circle the words that begin with a consonant cluster.

1. blow
2. grow
3. know
4. low
5. own
6. row
7. slow
8. snow
9. throw
10. tow

Challenge

Draw a Shape Box around each letter:

b e l o w　　m o w i n g　　s n o w m a n

Words with /ō/

Lesson 11

C Hide and Seek

Name ______________________________

Circle a cookie for each word you spell correctly.

D Other Word Forms

Using the words below, follow the instructions given by your teacher.

throws	mowed	owner	lowest	knows
throwing	blowing	snows	growing	
towed	rows	snowed	slower	
mow	owns	snowing	slowest	
mows	owned	lower	slowing	

E Fun Ways to Spell

Initial the box of each activity you finish.

1. 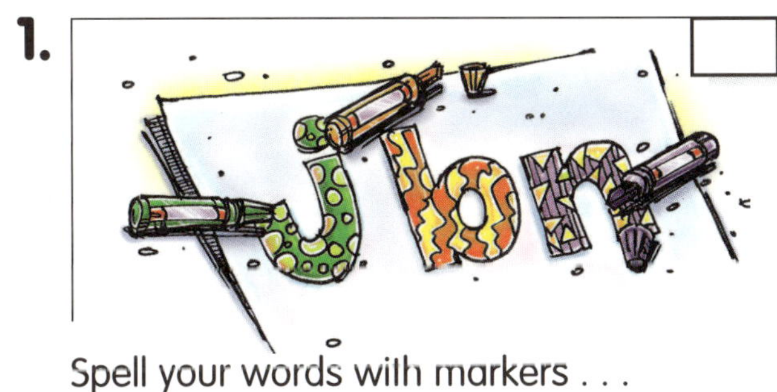

Spell your words with markers . . .

2. 

Spell your words with letter tiles . . .

3. 

Spell your words with snapping . . .

4. 

Spell your words with finger paint . . .

Words with /ō/

Lesson 11

Words with /ō/

Lesson 11

F Unscramble Words

Name ____________________

Change the scrambled letters to write your spelling words in the blanks. Trace Beth's path through Grandpa's flower garden by following your scrambled spelling words.

1. ________ woGr flowers.
2. ________ Do you won a pickup?
3. ________ The counter is not owl.
4. ________ Hill's pickup is not wslo.
5. ________ I owkn Jesus loves you.
6. ________ Dust will lobw across the field.
7. ________ hTorw the seeds on the ground.
8. ________ wSno is cold and white.
9. ________ Grandpa's tools were in a orw.
10. ________ wTo the pickup back to the farm.

Word Bank

blow	know	own	slow	throw
grow	low	row	snow	tow

G Dictation

Name ______________________

Listen and write the missing words.

1. Show ____ ____ ____ ____ ____ ____.

2. ____ ____ ____ ____ ____ plant ____ ____?

3. Tommy ____ ____ ____ bubble ____ ____ ____.

4. ____ ____ shovel ____ ____ ____.

H Proofreading

One word in each set is misspelled. Fill in the oval by the misspelled word.

1. ○ best ○ thro ○ blow

2. ○ slow ○ row ○ jrow

3. ○ cry ○ kno ○ road

4. ○ digit ○ kid ○ sno

5. ○ oan ○ number ○ tow

6. ○ men ○ loe ○ light

★ ○ sleep ○ child ○ beelo

★ ○ Bible ○ mowig ○ job

★ ○ wrote ○ gym ○ snoman

I Game

Name ______________________________

Take a walk with Beth as she enjoys memories of times shared with her grandpa. Move one space for each word you or your team spell correctly from this week's word list.

Start

Remember: No matter what happens, God never changes.

J Journaling

Write about a time you felt very sad.

A Test-Words

Name ______________________

Write each spelling word on the line as your teacher says it.

1. ______________________ 6. ______________________

2. ______________________ 7. ______________________

3. ______________________ 8. ______________________

4. ______________________ 9. ______________________

5. ______________________ 10. ______________________

Review Lesson 12

B Test-Sentences

The two underlined words in each of the sentences are misspelled. Write the sentences on the lines below, spelling each underlined word correctly.

I wil help cleen out the garage.

1. ______________________

There are mor cookies to baek.

2. ______________________

Did yu gro an inch this year?

3. ______________________

☆ Test-Challenge Words

Write each challenge word as your teacher says it.

Review

Lesson 12

C Test-Dictation

Name ______________________

Listen and write the missing words.

1. __________ going __________ __________

__________ __________.

2. __________ __________ __________ __________ __________

__________ __________ __________.

3. __________ __________ __________ __________ __________ __________.

D Test-Proofreading

One word in each set is misspelled. Fill in the oval by the misspelled word.

1. ○ oald
   ○ light
   ○ throw

2. ○ gaim
   ○ boat
   ○ gate

3. ○ snow
   ○ flie
   ○ read

4. ○ grade
   ○ might
   ○ toald

5. ○ loe
   ○ late
   ○ tree

6. ○ I'm
   ○ people
   ○ nam

7. ○ tye
   ○ tow
   ○ road

8. ○ gave
   ○ rolle
   ○ we'll

9. ○ slow
   ○ oane
   ○ east

☆ Test-Challenge Words

Write each challenge word as your teacher says it.

E Test-Shapes

Name ______________________________

Color each train car on which the word is spelled incorrectly.

☆ Test-Challenge Words

Write each challenge word as your teacher says it.

F Game

Name ______________________________

God made corn and grapes, and there are lots of things we can make out of them like corn flakes, corn chips, and raisins. Use these as your team names for this game. Place a sticker each time you or your team spell a review word correctly.

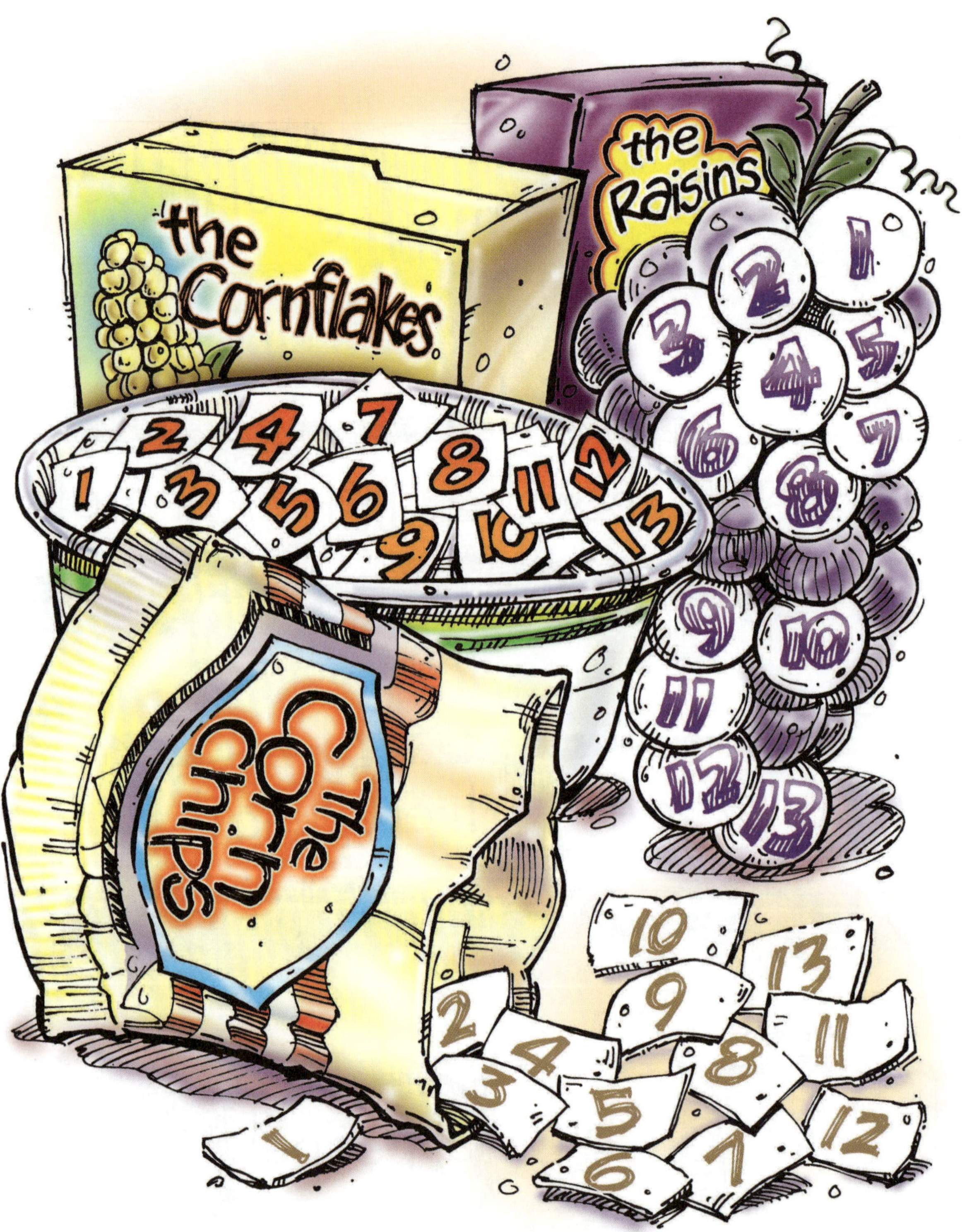

Remember: Choose to use for good the wonderful things God has made.

G Test-Words

Name ______________________

Write each spelling word on the line as your teacher says it.

1. ______________________ 6. ______________________

2. ______________________ 7. ______________________

3. ______________________ 8. ______________________

4. ______________________ 9. ______________________

5. ______________________ 10. ______________________

Review Lesson 12

H Test-Sentences

The two underlined words in each of the sentences are misspelled. Write the sentences on the lines below, spelling each underlined word correctly.

I can <u>ried</u> my bike on this <u>raod</u>.

1. ____

The sky was a deep <u>bloo</u> last <u>nite</u>.

2. ____

You may take the <u>bal</u> <u>hoam</u>.

3. ____

☆ Test-Challenge Words

Write each challenge word as your teacher says it.

I Writing Assessment

Name ______________________________

Write about why it is important for you to make good choices about what you put in your body.

____

____

____

____

____

____

____

____

____

Scripture

John 1:3

This certificate is awarded to:

____

for practicing the following words, doing terrific spelling activities and playing great spelling games!

Date __________________________

bake	be	buy	boat	blow
cake	clean	cry	cold	grow
came	east	dry	hold	know
game	even	fly	home	low
gate	he's	I'm	hope	own
gave	keep	light	most	row
grade	people	might	old	slow
late	read	night	road	snow
name	tree	right	roll	throw
page	we'll	tie	told	tow
★ break	★ between	★ Bible	★ don't	★ below
★ great	★ Jesus	★ child	★ over	★ mowing
★ obey	★ sleep	★ high	★ wrote	★ snowman

Dear Parent,

We are about to begin a new spelling unit containing five weekly lessons. A set of ten words plus three challenge words will be studied each week. All the words will be reviewed in the sixth week.

Values, based on each Scripture listed below, will be featured in that week's lesson.

Lesson 13	Lesson 14	Lesson 15	Lesson 16	Lesson 17
paint	arm	air	bird	any
pay	barn	bear	circle	baby
plays	car	eye	color	every
pray	card	fine	first	family
rain	dark	fire	purple	holy
say	far	like	under	only
stay	farm	line	water	penny
today	hard	their	were	ready
train	part	where	word	story
way	yard	write	work	very
☆ birthday	☆ heart	☆ beside	☆ heard	☆ city
☆ praise	☆ large	☆ care	☆ third	☆ easy
☆ stayed	☆ party	☆ while	☆ world	☆ study
Matt. 16:24	Luke 6:37	John 18:37	Luke 4:8	Luke 1:68

A Preview

Name ____________________

Write each word as your teacher says it.

1. ____________________
2. ____________________
3. ____________________
4. ____________________
5. ____________________
6. ____________________
7. ____________________
8. ____________________
9. ____________________
10. ____________________

Challenge Words

 ____________________

★ ____________________

★ ____________________

Scripture

Matthew 16:24

B Word Shapes

Name ____________________

Write each word in the correct Word Shape Box. Then, in the Word Shape Boxes, color the letters that spell the sound of /ā/ in each word. Circle the words that begin with a consonant cluster.

1. paint
2. pay
3. plays
4. pray
5. rain
6. say
7. stay
8. today
9. train
10. way

Words with /ā/

Lesson 13

Challenge

Draw a Shape Box around each letter:

birthday praise stayed

C Hide and Seek

Name ______________________________

Circle a cookie for each word you spell correctly.

D Other Word Forms

Using the words below, follow the instructions given by your teacher.

birthdays	paid	praised	rains	saying
paints	paying	praising	rained	stays
painted	played	prays	raining	stayed
painting	playing	prayed	rainy	staying
painter	player	praying	says	trains
pays	praises	prayer	said	ways

E Fun Ways to Spell

Initial the box of each activity you finish.

1. 

Spell your words with crayon . . .

3. 

Spell your words with rhythm instruments . . .

2. 

Spell your words with stencils . . .

4. 

Spell your words with cotton balls . . .

Words with /ā/

Lesson 13

F ABC Order

Name ______________________

Write each set of spelling words in alphabetical order.

1. plays, say, rain ________ ________ ________
2. way, train, pray ________ ________ ________
3. stay, pay, today ________ ________ ________
4. rain, paint, way ________ ________ ________
5. train, stay, plays ________ ________ ________
6. way, today, pray ________ ________ ________
7. paint, say, rain ________ ________ ________
8. way, train, pay ________ ________ ________
9. say, plays, today ________ ________ ________
10. rain, paint, stay ________ ________ ________

a b c d e f g h i j k l m n o p q r s t u v w x y z

A B C D E F G H I J K L M N O P Q R S T U V W X Y Z

G Dictation

Name ______________________

Listen and write the missing words.

1. ________ want ______ ________ ________ ________ ________.

2. ________ farmers ________ ________ ________.

3. Rosa ______ ______ ____ ______ ______ ______.

4. Which ________ ________ ________ ________ ______ ______?

H Proofreading

One word in each set is misspelled. Fill in the oval by the misspelled word.

1. ○ page ○ paitn ○ way
2. ○ sey ○ know ○ clean
3. ○ pray ○ keep ○ playz
4. ○ grow ○ stay ○ tooday
5. ○ trane ○ what ○ most
6. ○ people ○ rane ○ pay

★ ○ staed ○ Bible ○ gym

★ ○ don't ○ below ○ praez

★ ○ wrote ○ berthday ○ high

I Game

Name ______________________________

Tommy and Lisa's dad made stew for supper while their mom was away helping their grandmother. Be the first to the dinner table by moving one space each time you or your team spell a word correctly from this week's word list.

Remember: Follow Jesus by doing what He would do.

J Journaling

Write a promise to God about how you will

A Preview

Name ______________________________

Write each word as your teacher says it.

1. ______________________
2. ______________________
3. ______________________
4. ______________________
5. ______________________
6. ______________________
7. ______________________
8. ______________________
9. ______________________
10. ______________________

Challenge Words

★ ______________________

★ ______________________

★ ______________________

Scripture

Luke 6:37

B Word Shapes

Name ___________________________

Write each word in the correct Word Shape Box. Then, in the Word Shape Boxes, color the letters that spell the sound of **/är/** in each word.

1. arm
2. barn
3. car
4. card
5. dark
6. far
7. farm
8. hard
9. part
10. yard

Challenge

Draw a Shape Box around each letter:

heart large party

Words with /är/

Lesson 14

C Hide and Seek

Name ______________________________

Circle a cookie for each word you spell correctly.

D Other Word Forms

Using the words below, follow the instructions given by your teacher.

arms	cars	farms	hardly	parted
armed	darker	farmed	hearts	parting
armful	darkest	farming	larger	parties
barns	farther	harder	largest	impart
cards	farthest	hardest	parts	yards

E Fun Ways to Spell

Initial the box of each activity you finish.

1. 

Spell your words with an eraser . . .

2. 

Spell your words with paint . . .

3. 

Spell your words with clapping . . .

4. 

Spell your words in damp sand . . .

F Rhyme Time

Name ______________________

Write spelling words, from your Word Bank, that rhyme with the words above each blank line.

Word Bank

arm	car	dark	farm	part
barn	card	far	hard	yard

G Dictation

Name ______________________

Listen and write the missing words.

1. ________ ________ ________ ________ ________

________ ________ ________ ________.

2. ________ can't ________ ________ ________

________ ________ ________ ________.

3. ________ ________ ________ ________ ________

________ ________ here?

H Proofreading

One word in each set is misspelled. Fill in the oval by the misspelled word.

1. ◯ say
   ◯ own
   ◯ darck

2. ◯ today
   ◯ harb
   ◯ far

3. ◯ east
   ◯ qart
   ◯ tow

4. ◯ yarb
   ◯ arm
   ◯ boat

5. ◯ kar
   ◯ rain
   ◯ barn

6. ◯ might
   ◯ kard
   ◯ farm

★ ◯ partie
   ◯ over
   ◯ sleep

★ ◯ praise
   ◯ snowman
   ◯ larj

★ ◯ mowing
   ◯ haert
   ◯ stayed

I Game

Name ______________________________

Kristin wants to apologize to Setsuko for her unkind words. Lead the way by moving one space each time you or your team spell a word correctly from this week's word list.

START

Remember: Before you say something
unkind, think how you would feel
if the unkind words were about you.

J Journaling

follow Him even when it is not easy to do.
What do you think Kristin should do about
hurting Setsuko's feelings? Write down your ideas.

A Preview

Name ______________________

Write each word as your teacher says it.

1. ______________________
2. ______________________
3. ______________________
4. ______________________
5. ______________________
6. ______________________
7. ______________________
8. ______________________
9. ______________________
10. ______________________

Challenge Words

 ______________________

 ______________________

☆ ______________________

Scripture

John 18:37

B Word Shapes

Name ______________________________

Write each word in the correct Word Shape Boxes. Then, in the Word Shape Boxes, color the letters that spell the sound of **/âr/** or **/ī/** in each word. Circle the words that begin with the digraph **th** or **wh**.

1. air
2. bear
3. eye
4. fine
5. fire
6. like
7. line
8. their
9. where
10. write

Challenge

Draw a Shape Box around each letter:

b e s i d e   c a r e   w h i l e

C Hide and Seek

Name ______________________

Circle a cookie for each word you spell correctly.

D Other Word Forms

Using the words below, follow the instructions given by your teacher.

aired	cares	fines	likes	theirs
airs	cared	fined	liked	writer
airing	caring	fining	liking	writing
bears	eyes	fires	lines	writes
bearing	eyed	fired	lined	
besides	eyeing	firing	lining	

E Fun Ways to Spell

Initial the box of each activity you finish.

1.

Spell your words with puzzles . . .

2.

Spell your words on a paper chain . . .

3.

Spell your words out loud . . .

4.

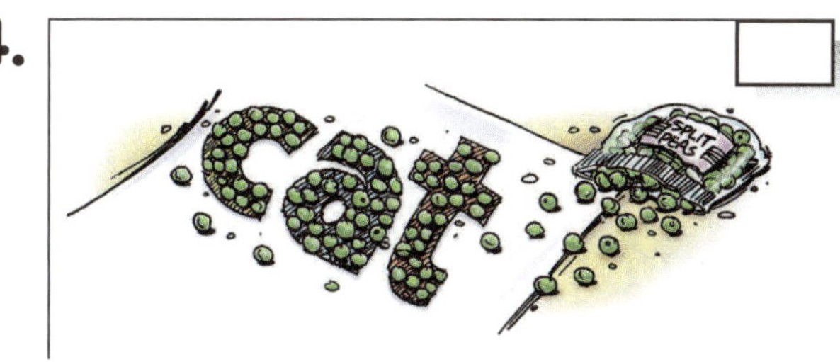

Spell your words with split peas . . .

Words with /âr/ or /ī/

Lesson 15

F Word Change

Name ______________________

Write a spelling word in place of the underlined word or words.

1. All the desks were in a row. ____________
2. The brown furry animal is cute and mean. ____________
3. Tony and Stephen's favorite game is dodge ball. ____________

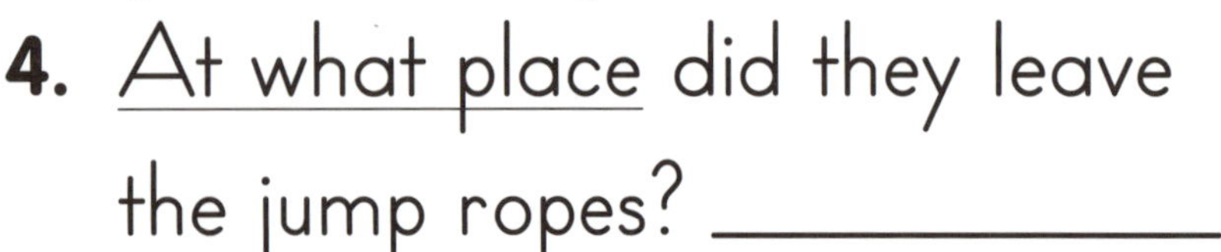

4. At what place did they leave the jump ropes? ____________

5. Print your name here. ____________
6. It is always okay to tell the truth. ____________
7. The ball flew through what we breathe. ____________
8. Tony did not want to look Mrs. Morgan in the seeing part of her face. ____________
9. Lies grow like a wild red hot flame. ____________
10. Tony does not enjoy eating carrots. ____________

☆ At the same time he played, everyone ate lunch. ____________

☆ She will mind if you leave the ropes out. ____________

☆ The trash can was next to the door. ____________

Word Bank

air	eye	fire	line	where	☆ beside	☆ while
bear	fine	like	their	write	☆ care	

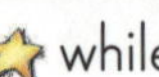

G Dictation

Name ______________________

Listen and write the missing words.

1. Sarah _______ _______ _______ _______ letters.

2. _______ _______ _______ _______ _______ _______.

3. Grandpa built _______ _______ _______ _______ _______.

4. _______ _______ _______ coats?

H Proofreading

One word in each set is misspelled. Fill in the oval by the misspelled word.

1. ⬭ kid
   ⬭ dark
   ⬭ ther

2. ⬭ road
   ⬭ ayr
   ⬭ stay

3. ⬭ wriet
   ⬭ tree
   ⬭ line

4. ⬭ hard
   ⬭ baer
   ⬭ eye

5. ⬭ number
   ⬭ fier
   ⬭ cold

6. ⬭ wher
   ⬭ fine
   ⬭ paint

★ ⬭ large
  ⬭ beeside
  ⬭ stayed

★ ⬭ cair
  ⬭ party
  ⬭ forgot

★ ⬭ heart
  ⬭ whiel
  ⬭ between

I Game

Name ______________________________

Tony wants to obey the class rule and take home the part of his lunch he did not eat. Help Tony get his uneaten lunch out of the trash can. Move one space for each word you or your team spells correctly.

Remember: Honesty shows you love Jesus.

J Journaling

Make a list of people whom you can trust to always tell the truth. Label the list: **Truth Lovers**.

A Preview

Name ________________

Write each word as your teacher says it.

1. ________________

2. ________________

3. ________________

4. ________________

5. ________________

6. ________________

7. ________________

8. ________________

9. ________________

10. ________________

Challenge Words

☆ ________________

☆ ________________

☆ ________________

Scripture

Luke 4:8

B Word Shapes

Name ______________________

Write each word in the correct Word Shape Boxes. Then, in the Word Shape Boxes, color the letters that spell the sound of **/ûr/** or **/ər/** in each word. Circle the words which have two syllables.

1. bird
2. circle
3. color
4. first
5. purple
6. under
7. water
8. were
9. word
10. work

Challenge

Draw a Shape Box around each letter:

heard   third   world

C Hide and Seek

Name ______________________________

Circle a cookie for each word you spell correctly.

D Other Word Forms

Using the words below, follow the instructions given by your teacher.

birds	colors	thirds	words	worked
circles	colored	waters	worded	working
circled	coloring	watered	wording	worlds
circling	purples	watering	works	

E Fun Ways to Spell

Initial the box of each activity you finish.

1. 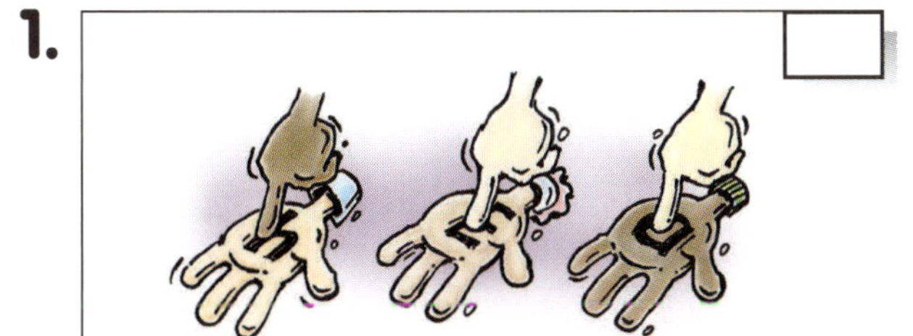

Spell your words in your classmate's hand . . .

2. 

Spell your words with paper cups . . .

3. 

Spell your words out of the letter box . . .

4. 

Spell your words with shaving cream . . .

F Letter Change

Name ____________________

Change the underlined letter or letters, and write the spelling word in the blank.

1. Sarah's eyes there wet. __________
2. The girls were in a circus around Katelynn's desk. __________

3. The Bible is God's cord. __________
4. The third is in its cage. __________
5. Keep God thirst in your life. __________

6. Drink lots of later every day. __________
7. The cover of Katie's hair is black. __________
8. They will fork for the kids in Malawi. __________
9. The dancing dragon tunic is not puddle. __________
10. Sarah had dirt wonder her fingernails. __________

★ Girls all over the works love dolls. __________

★ Katelynn is thirst. __________

★ She beard Katelynn liked dolls. __________

Word Bank

bird	color	purple	water	word	★ heard	★ world
circle	first	under	were	work	★ third	

G Dictation

Name ______________________

Listen and write the missing words.

1. ________ ________ ________ built ________ ________ ________.

2. Please ________ ________ ________ ________.

3. Stephen, ________ ________ swimming ________ ________ ________?

H Proofreading

One word in each set is misspelled. Fill in the oval by the misspelled word.

1. ◯ coler ◯ train ◯ say
2. ◯ work ◯ purpel ◯ yard
3. ◯ woter ◯ often ◯ jump
4. ◯ their ◯ were ◯ werd
5. ◯ farm ◯ like ◯ berd
6. ◯ sirkel ◯ first ◯ under

★ ◯ wirld ◯ while ◯ party

★ ◯ heart ◯ thirb ◯ birthday

★ ◯ child ◯ haerd ◯ once

I Game

Name ______________________________

Place a game piece over each word your teacher says and spells. If the word appears on your card more than once, place a game piece over only one of the words. When you get five game pieces in a row, raise your hand and say, "Spelling is fun!"

		FREE		

Remember: Love and obey God.

J Journaling

Make a list just like Mrs. Morgan's class did in the story. Label the list: **Things I Like To Do**.

A Preview

Name ______________________

Write each word as your teacher says it.

1. ______________________

2. ______________________

3. ______________________

4. ______________________

5. ______________________

6. ______________________

7. ______________________

8. ______________________

9. ______________________

10. ______________________

Challenge Words

★ ______________________

★ ______________________

★ ______________________

Scripture

Luke 1:68

B Word Shapes

Name ______________________________

Write each word in the correct Word Shape Boxes. Then, in the Word Shape Boxes, color the letter that spells the sound of **/ē/** in each word. Circle the words which have two syllables. Draw a line under the words which have three syllables.

1. any
2. baby
3. every
4. family
5. holy
6. only
7. penny
8. ready
9. story
10. very

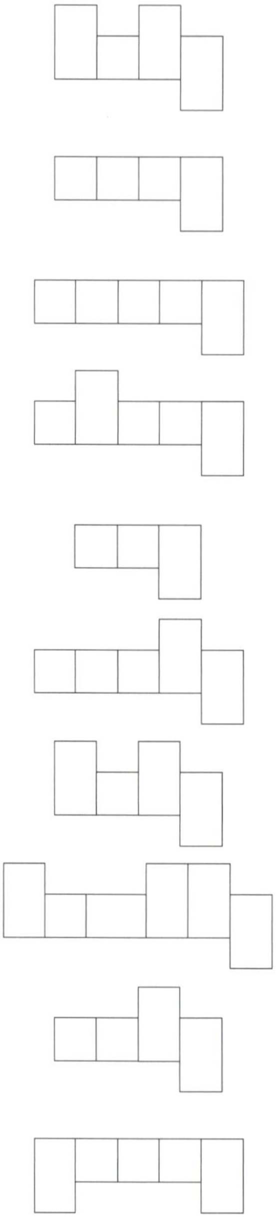

Challenge

Draw a Shape Box around each letter:

city easy study

C Hide and Seek

Name ______________________

Circle a cookie for each word you spell correctly.

D Other Word Forms

Using the words below, follow the instructions given by your teacher.

babies	easiest	holiest	readiest
cities	families	pennies	stories
easier	holier	readier	studies

E Fun Ways to Spell

Initial the box of each activity you finish.

1. 

Spell your words with markers . . .

2. 

Spell your words with letter tiles . . .

3. 

Spell your words with snapping . . .

4. 

Spell your words with finger paint . . .

Words with y as /ē/

Lesson 17

F Sentence Order

Name ______________________

Place each set of word groups in order to write a sentence. Circle the spelling words.

all came.  family  Our

1. ______________________

story.  ready  We are for a

2. ______________________

our  about God.  It is  holy

3. ______________________

only one  I have  penny.

4. ______________________

The  very  big.  not  baby is

5. ______________________

ice cream?  any  Is there

6. ______________________

wrapped.  gift is  Every

7. ______________________

Word Bank

any	every	holy	penny	story
baby	family	only	ready	very

G Dictation

Name ______________________

Listen and write the missing words.

1. ______ ______ ______ ______ ______ ______.

2. ______ ______ brought ______ food.

3. ______ ______ ______ ______ ______ ______ ______ party yet?

4. Daniel ______ ______ ______ ______ ______.

H Proofreading

One word in each set is misspelled. Fill in the oval by the misspelled word.

1. ◯ baby ◯ peny ◯ bear

2. ◯ color ◯ story ◯ iny

3. ◯ evry ◯ pray ◯ very

4. ◯ holy ◯ air ◯ reddy

5. ◯ ownly ◯ water ◯ part

6. ◯ snow ◯ famly ◯ train

★ ◯ over ◯ ezy ◯ great

★ ◯ bath ◯ sity ◯ mowing

★ ◯ Jesus ◯ stuby ◯ apple

I Game

Name ______________________________

Help Setsuko find Chimi. Color one space for each word you or your team spell correctly from this week's word list.

Remember: God loved you so much,
He sent Jesus to save you.

J Journaling

Finish this message to God: **Thank You for . . .**
I praise You because . . . When I feel lost I will . . .
I know You love me because . . .

A Test-Words

Name ______________________

Write each spelling word on the line as your teacher says it.

1. ______________________ 6. ______________________

2. ______________________ 7. ______________________

3. ______________________ 8. ______________________

4. ______________________ 9. ______________________

5. ______________________ 10. ______________________

B Test-Sentences

The two underlined words in each of the sentences are misspelled. Write the sentences on the lines below, spelling each underlined word correctly.

Each dey she plaez with me.

1. ____

Put som sand in thier bucket.

2. ____

Let's all sitt in a sirkle.

3. ____

☆ Test-Challenge Words

Write each challenge word as your teacher says it.

C Test-Dictation

Name ______________________________

Listen and write the missing words.

1. _____ _______ _________ ________ _______ ________.

2. _________ __________ ____________ __________?

3. ____________ ______ _________ birthday.

Review

Lesson 18

D Test-Proofreading

One word in each set is misspelled.
Fill in the oval by the misspelled word.

1. ○ ferst
   ○ farm
   ○ purple

2. ○ work
   ○ penny
   ○ evry

3. ○ water
   ○ stae
   ○ holy

4. ○ darck
   ○ pay
   ○ fine

5. ○ card
   ○ coler
   ○ train

6. ○ farr
   ○ work
   ○ were

7. ○ penny
   ○ part
   ○ iye

8. ○ werd
   ○ way
   ○ yard

9. ○ ownli
   ○ fire
   ○ like

☆ Test-Challenge Words

Write each challenge word as your teacher says it.

E Test-Shapes

Name ______________________

Color each bike helmet on which the word is spelled incorrectly.

Test-Challenge Words

Write each challenge word as your teacher says it.

F Game

Name ______________________________

Stephen got hit by a car while crossing the street on his bike. A lot of people helped Stephen when he got hurt. Use some of them as your team names for this game. Place a sticker each time you or your team correctly spell a review word.

Remember: Even when bad things happen, God is always there.

Review

Lesson 18

G Test-Words

Name ______________________

Write each spelling word on the line as your teacher says it.

1. ______________________ 6. ______________________

2. ______________________ 7. ______________________

3. ______________________ 8. ______________________

4. ______________________ 9. ______________________

5. ______________________ 10. ______________________

H Test-Sentences

The two underlined words in each of the sentences are misspelled. Write the sentences on the lines below, spelling each underlined word correctly.

Dad was hapie to read the stori.

1. ____

muthir has dinner redy for us.

2. ____

The broun leaf is veri brittle.

3. ____

Test-Challenge Words

Write each challenge word as your teacher says it.

Review Lesson 18

I Writing Assessment

Name ______________________________

Make a list of bicycle safety rules. Label your list: **Bicycle Safety**.
Below your list, draw a picture of a bicycle accident you had or saw happen.

____

1. ____

2. ____

3. ____

4. ____

5. ____

Review

Lesson 18

Scripture

Matthew 28:20

This certificate is awarded to:

____

for practicing the following words, doing terrific spelling activities and playing great spelling games!

Date __________________________

- paint
- pay
- plays
- pray
- rain
- say
- stay
- today
- train
- way
- ☆ birthday
- ☆ praise
- ☆ stayed

- arm
- barn
- car
- card
- dark
- far
- farm
- hard
- part
- yard
- ☆ heart
- ☆ large
- ☆ party

- air
- bear
- eye
- fine
- fire
- like
- line
- their
- where
- write
- ☆ beside
- ☆ care
- ☆ while

- bird
- circle
- color
- first
- purple
- under
- water
- were
- word
- work
- ☆ heard
- ☆ third
- ☆ world

- any
- baby
- every
- family
- holy
- only
- penny
- ready
- story
- very
- ☆ city
- ☆ easy
- ☆ study

Dear Parent,

We are about to begin a new spelling unit containing five weekly lessons. A set of ten words plus three challenge words will be studied each week. All the words will be reviewed in the sixth week.

Values, based on each Scripture listed below, will be featured in that week's lesson.

Lesson 19	Lesson 20	Lesson 21	Lesson 22	Lesson 23
books	food	around	boys	also
could	new	bow	door	always
dear	noon	count	enjoy	children
ear	room	cow	form	draw
full	soon	found	horse	each
hear	too	house	Lord	small
here	tooth	round	noise	such
took	use	sound	orange	walk
wood	who	south	store	want
would	zoo	vowel	toy	which
☆ looked	☆ balloon	☆ cloud	☆ before	☆ called
☆ stood	☆ knew	☆ crown	☆ important	☆ lunch
☆ year	☆ through	☆ flower	☆ voice	☆ wanted
Matthew 6:34	Luke 15:10	Mark 4:23,24	Luke 11:13	Luke 11:28

Name ______________________

A Preview

Write each word as your teacher says it.

1. ______________________
2. ______________________
3. ______________________
4. ______________________
5. ______________________
6. ______________________
7. ______________________
8. ______________________
9. ______________________
10. ______________________

Challenge Words

★ ______________________

Scripture

Matthew 6:34

B Word Shapes

Name ______________________________

Write each word in the correct Word Shape Boxes. Then, in the Word Shape Boxes, color the letter or letters that spell the sound of /îr/ or /ů/ in each word. Circle the words in which /ů/ is spelled with **ou.**

1. books
2. could
3. dear
4. ear
5. full
6. hear
7. here
8. took
9. wood
10. would

Challenge

Draw a Shape Box around each letter:

looked   stood   year

C Hide and Seek

Name ______________________________

Circle a cookie for each word you spell correctly.

D Other Word Forms

Using the words below, follow the instructions given by your teacher.

book	dearest	fuller	looking
booked	dearly	hears	wooden
booking	ears	look	years
dears	fullest	looks	

E Fun Ways to Spell

Initial the box of each activity you finish.

1. 

Spell your words with crayon . . .

3. 

Spell your words with rhythm instruments . . .

2. 

Spell your words with stencils . . .

4. 

Spell your words with cotton balls . . .

F ABC Order

Name ____________________

Write each set of spelling words in alphabetical order.

1. would ____________
   full ____________
   ear ____________
   took ____________

2. dear ____________
   books ____________
   could ____________
   here ____________

3. took ____________
   wood ____________
   hear ____________
   dear ____________

★ stood ____________
   year ____________
   looked ____________
   lamp ____________

A B C D E F G H I J K L M N O P Q R S T U V W X Y Z

a b c d e f g h i j k l m n o p q r s t u v w x y z

G Dictation

Name ____________________

Listen and write the missing words.

1. Rosa's basket ____ ____ ____ ____.

2. ____ ____ ____ ____ calling?

3. ____ ____ ____ ____ ____ ____ need.

4. Who ____ my ____ muffs?

Words with /îr/ or /ü/

Lesson 19

H Proofreading

One word in each set is misspelled. Fill in the oval by the misspelled word.

1. ◯ ready
   ◯ could
   ◯ daer

2. ◯ ful
   ◯ throw
   ◯ family

3. ◯ work
   ◯ woob
   ◯ books

4. ◯ into
   ◯ heer
   ◯ arm

5. ◯ took
   ◯ penny
   ◯ woud

6. ◯ eer
   ◯ here
   ◯ fire

★ ◯ third
  ◯ stoob
  ◯ while

★ ◯ city
  ◯ lookt
  ◯ study

★ ◯ yeer
  ◯ care
  ◯ world

I Game

Name ______________________________

Sign Stephen's cast. Each time a person on your team spells a word correctly from this week's word list, write their name on Stephen's cast.

Remember: Only God is able to take care of tomorrow. Choose not to worry.

J Journaling

Write: **Things I Worry About**.
Make a list of things that worry you.
At the bottom of the page, Write: **God will take care of my tomorrows**.

A Preview

Name ______________________

Write each word as your teacher says it.

1. ______________________
2. ______________________
3. ______________________
4. ______________________
5. ______________________
6. ______________________
7. ______________________
8. ______________________
9. ______________________
10. ______________________

Challenge Words

★ ______________________

★ ______________________

★ ______________________

Scripture

Luke 15:10

B Word Shapes

Name ______________________________

Write each word in the correct Word Shape Boxes. Then, in the Word Shape Boxes, color the letter or letters that spell the sound of /ü/ or /ū/ in each word. Circle the word which has the sound of /ū/.

1. food
2. new
3. noon
4. room
5. soon
6. too
7. tooth
8. use
9. who
10. zoo

Challenge

Draw a Shape Box around each letter:

balloon knew through

C Hide and Seek

Name ___________________________

Circle a cookie for each word you spell correctly.

D Other Word Forms

Using the words below, follow the instructions given by your teacher.

balloons	newest	roomiest	who's
foods	rooms	sooner	zoos
news	roomy	soonest	
newer	roomier	used	

E Fun Ways to Spell

Initial the box of each activity you finish.

1. 

Spell your words with an eraser . . .

2. 

Spell your words with paint . . .

3. 

Spell your words with clapping . . .

4. 

Spell your words in damp sand . . .

Words with /ü/ or /ū/

Lesson 20

F Clues

Name ______________________

Use the clues to write the spelling words.

1. Place animals live: __________
2. Something to eat: __________
3. Middle of the day: __________
4. ______ lost twenty dollars?
5. Not a long time: ________
6. I have a __________ pad of paper.
7. You may not _________ my pad!
8. He stared out the window of his _________.
9. Your front one may have fallen out: _________
10. You can choose to repent, _________.

★ Christopher _________ he should not yell at Cory.

★ Something you can pop: _________

★ Christopher was _________ with his job at school.

Word Bank

food	noon	soon	tooth	who	★ balloon	★ through
new	room	too	use	zoo	★ knew	

G Dictation

Name ______________________

Listen and write the missing words.

1. ________ ____ __________ ________ ________ ________ _____ ________.

2. _______ _______ ______ ______ _____ ______ ______ _____ _______.

3. _______ ______ ______ ______ _____ camera?

4. ______ ______ lose ____ ______, _____?

H Proofreading

One word in each set is misspelled. Fill in the oval by the misspelled word.

1. ⬭ noon
   ⬭ story
   ⬭ tooht

2. ⬭ ear
   ⬭ room
   ⬭ foob

3. ⬭ very
   ⬭ too
   ⬭ nuw

4. ⬭ only
   ⬭ zu
   ⬭ baby

5. ⬭ hoo
   ⬭ wood
   ⬭ soon

6. ⬭ uze
   ⬭ fine
   ⬭ far

★ ⬭ stood
   ⬭ third
   ⬭ thru

★ ⬭ baloon
   ⬭ easy
   ⬭ job

★ ⬭ because
   ⬭ sentence
   ⬭ knuw

I Game

Name ______________________________

Christopher wants to return the money he found. Lead the way to the school office by moving one space each time you or your team spell a word correctly from this week's word list.

Remember: Angels sing for joy when you ask for God's forgiveness!

J Journaling

Write about something you did that was wrong. What did you do? How did you feel?

How do you think the angels felt when you made your mistake right?

A Preview

Name ______________________

Write each word as your teacher says it.

1. ______________________

2. ______________________

3. ______________________

4. ______________________

5. ______________________

6. ______________________

7. ______________________

8. ______________________

9. ______________________

10. ______________________

Challenge Words

☆ ______________________

☆ ______________________

☆ ______________________

Words with /ou/

Lesson 21

Scripture

Mark 4:23, 24

Words with /ou/

Lesson 21

B Word Shapes

Name ___________________________

Write each word in the correct Word Shape Boxes. Then, in the Word Shape Boxes, color the letters that spell the diphthong **/ou/** in each word. Circle the words in which the diphthong **/ou/** is spelled with **ow**.

1. around
2. bow
3. count
4. cow
5. found
6. house
7. round
8. sound
9. south
10. vowel

Challenge

Draw a Shape Box around each letter:

c l o u d   c r o w n   f l o w e r

C Hide and Seek

Name ________________________________

Circle a cookie for each word you spell correctly.

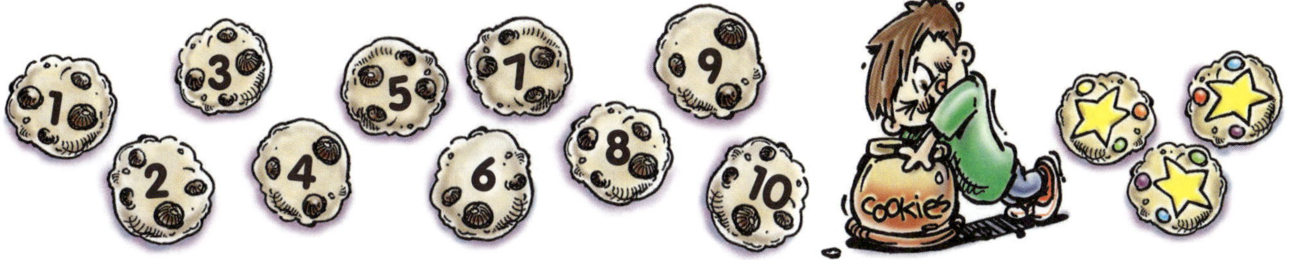

D Other Word Forms

Using the words below, follow the instructions given by your teacher.

bows	counting	flowering	roundest	vowels
bowed	cows	houses	rounding	
cloudy	crown	housed	sounds	
counts	flowers	housing	sounded	
counted	flowered	rounder	sounding	

E Fun Ways to Spell

Initial the box of each activity you finish.

1.

Spell your words with puzzles . . .

3.

Spell your words out loud . . .

2.

Spell your words on a paper chain . . .

4.

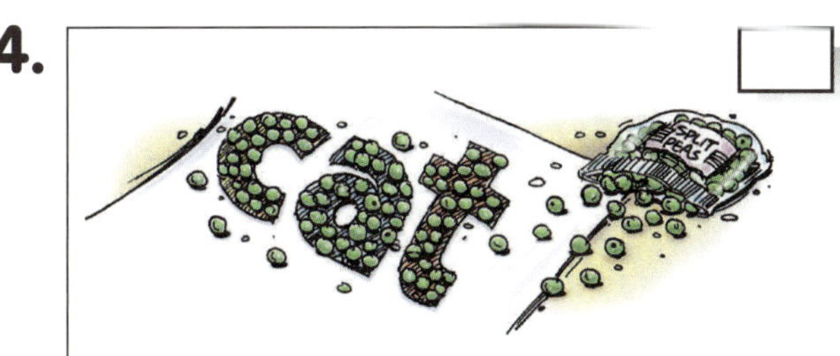

Spell your words with split peas . . .

F Words In Sentences

Name ____________________

Write the spelling word to complete each sentence.

1. The softball is __________.
2. It is warmer in the __________.
3. We learned what the __________ "o" says with "w".
4. There was a pleading __________ in Matthew's voice.
5. Alex __________ his glove at the taco place.
6. Go back in the __________ and get your jacket.
7. Don't __________ on winning every T-Ball game.
8. The boys stood __________ their coach.
9. The __________ stood in the field and ate grass.
10. Take a __________ after that fine catch.

☆ The __________ covered the sun.

☆ You will have stars in your __________.

☆ One __________ was blooming in the garden.

Word Bank

around	count	found	round	south	☆ cloud	☆ flower
bow	cow	house	sound	vowel	☆ crown	

Words with /ou/

Lesson 21

G Dictation

Name ________________

Listen and write the missing words.

1. ________ ________ walked ________ ________ ________.

2. ________ ______ birds flying ________.

3. ________ ________ needs ______ least ______ ________.

4. Stephen ________ ____ ________ dish.

H Proofreading

One word in each set is misspelled. Fill in the oval by the misspelled word.

1. ⬭ yard ⬭ zoo ⬭ fownd

2. ⬭ vowel ⬭ arownd ⬭ food

3. ⬭ souht ⬭ cow ⬭ could

4. ⬭ under ⬭ cownt ⬭ new

5. ⬭ sounb ⬭ ear ⬭ round

6. ⬭ hows ⬭ bow ⬭ here

★ ⬭ balloon ⬭ croun ⬭ stood

★ ⬭ through ⬭ clowd ⬭ stayed

★ ⬭ flowr ⬭ knew ⬭ looked

Words with /ou/

Lesson 21

I Game

Name ______________________________

Matthew and Alex each forgot something. Run home to find what they left behind. Color one space each time you spell a word correctly from this week's word list.

ALEX

START

MATTHEW

Remember: Listen carefully to what you are told to do and then do it carefully.

J Journaling

Design a sign telling kids to listen and follow directions.

A Preview

Name ______________________

Write each word as your teacher says it.

1. ______________________

2. ______________________

3. ______________________

4. ______________________

5. ______________________

6. ______________________

7. ______________________

8. ______________________

9. ______________________

10. ______________________

Challenge Words

 ______________________

 ______________________

★ ______________________

Scripture

Luke 11:13

B Word Shapes

Name ______________________________

Write each word in the correct Word Shape Boxes. Then, in the Word Shape Boxes, color the letters that spell the sound of **/ôr/** or the diphthong **/oi/** in each word. Circle the word in which **/ôr/** is spelled with **oor** .

1. boys
2. door
3. enjoy
4. form
5. horse
6. Lord
7. noise
8. orange
9. store
10. toy

Challenge

Draw a Shape Box around each letter:

before   important   voice

C Hide and Seek

Name ____________________

Circle a cookie for each word you spell correctly.

D Other Word Forms

Using the words below, follow the instructions given by your teacher.

boy	formed	noises	toys	voicing
doors	forming	noisy	toyed	
enjoys	horses	oranges	toying	
enjoyed	horsed	stores	unimportant	
enjoying	horsing	stored	voices	
forms	Lords	storing	voiced	

E Fun Ways to Spell

Initial the box of each activity you finish.

1.

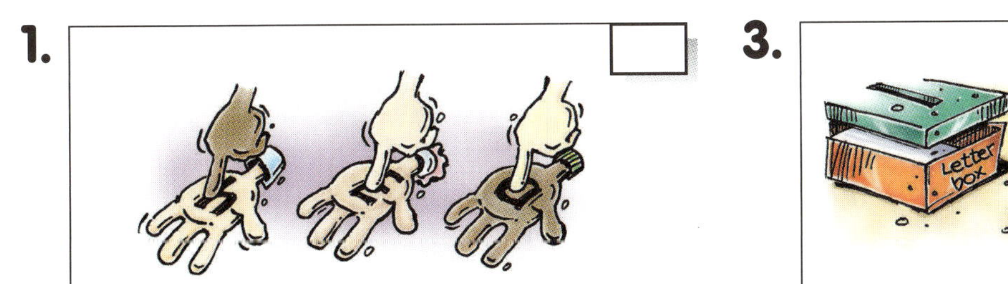

Spell your words in your classmate's hand . . .

3.

Spell your words out of the letter box . . .

2.

Spell your words with paper cups . . .

4.

Spell your words with shaving cream . . .

F Crossword

Name ______________________________

Use the puzzle clues to write the spelling words.

Across

3. open the ______
5. color
8. something to play with
9. to like
10 a place to buy things

Down

1. to shape
2. animal
4. God
6. loud sound
7. not girls but ______

1.
2.
3.
4.
5.
6.
7.
8.
9.
10.

Word Bank

boys	enjoy	horse	noise	store
door	form	Lord	orange	toy

Words with /oi/ or /ôr/

Lesson 22

G Dictation

Name ______________________

Listen and write the missing words.

1. _____ _____ _____ _____ _____ airplane.

2. Daniel led _____ _____ through _____ _____ _____.

3. _____ _____ _____ _____ _____ _____ _____ _____.

4. _____ _____ loves _____ _____ _____.

H Proofreading

One word in each set is misspelled. Fill in the oval by the misspelled word.

1. ◯ Lord
   ◯ dear
   ◯ engoy

2. ◯ hors
   ◯ took
   ◯ toy

3. ◯ first
   ◯ boyz
   ◯ where

4. ◯ noon
   ◯ store
   ◯ dor

5. ◯ circle
   ◯ line
   ◯ noiz

6. ◯ ornge
   ◯ baby
   ◯ form

★ ◯ flower
   ◯ importnt
   ◯ stood

★ ◯ crown
   ◯ befour
   ◯ through

★ ◯ easy
   ◯ vois
   ◯ year

I Game

Name ______________________

Place a game piece over each word your teacher says and spells. If the word appears on your card more than once, place a game piece over only one of the words. When you get five game pieces in a row, raise your hand and say, "Spelling is fun!"

		FREE		

Remember: God gives the Holy Spirit to guide us, but we have the choice to listen.

J Journaling

Write about a time you didn't know the right thing to do. Finish this sentence:
When I don't know what to do, I will . . .

A Preview

Name ______________________

Write each word as your teacher says it.

1. ______________________

2. ______________________

3. ______________________

4. ______________________

5. ______________________

6. ______________________

7. ______________________

8. ______________________

9. ______________________

10. ______________________

Challenge Words

 ______________________

★ ______________________

★ ______________________

Scripture

Luke 11:28

Words with /ô/ or /ch/

Lesson 23

B Word Shapes

Name ____________________

Write each word in the correct Word Shape Boxes. Then, in the Word Shape Boxes, color the letter or letters that spell the sound of **/ô/** or **/ch/** in each word. Circle the word which has two digraphs.

1. also
2. always
3. children
4. draw
5. each
6. small
7. such
8. walk
9. want
10. which

Challenge

Draw a Shape Box around each letter:

called   lunch   wanted

C Hide and Seek

Name ___________________________

Circle a cookie for each word you spell correctly.

D Other Word Forms

Using the words below, follow the instructions given by your teacher.

call	lunches	walks	wants
calling	smaller	walked	wanting
draws	smallest	walking	

E Fun Ways to Spell

Initial the box of each activity you finish.

1.

Spell your words with markers . . .

2.

Spell your words with letter tiles . . .

3.

Spell your words with snapping . . .

4.

Spell your words with finger paint . . .

Words with /ô/ or /ch/

Lesson 23

F Unscramble Words

Name ______________________

Use the underlined letters to write a spelling word.

1. ________ The lirdench made origami bunnies.
2. ________ They made hace one by folding paper.
3. ________ Setsuko laso made some baby bunnies.
4. ________ The baby bunnies were very mlasl.
5. ________ Can you wrad a picture of a bunny?
6. ________ We tanw to be kind to others.
7. ________ Some older people find it hard to lakw.
8. ________ Visiting them is hsuc a nice thing to do.
9. ________ Helping others is slawya a good choice.
10. ________ Wchih bunny do you like the best?

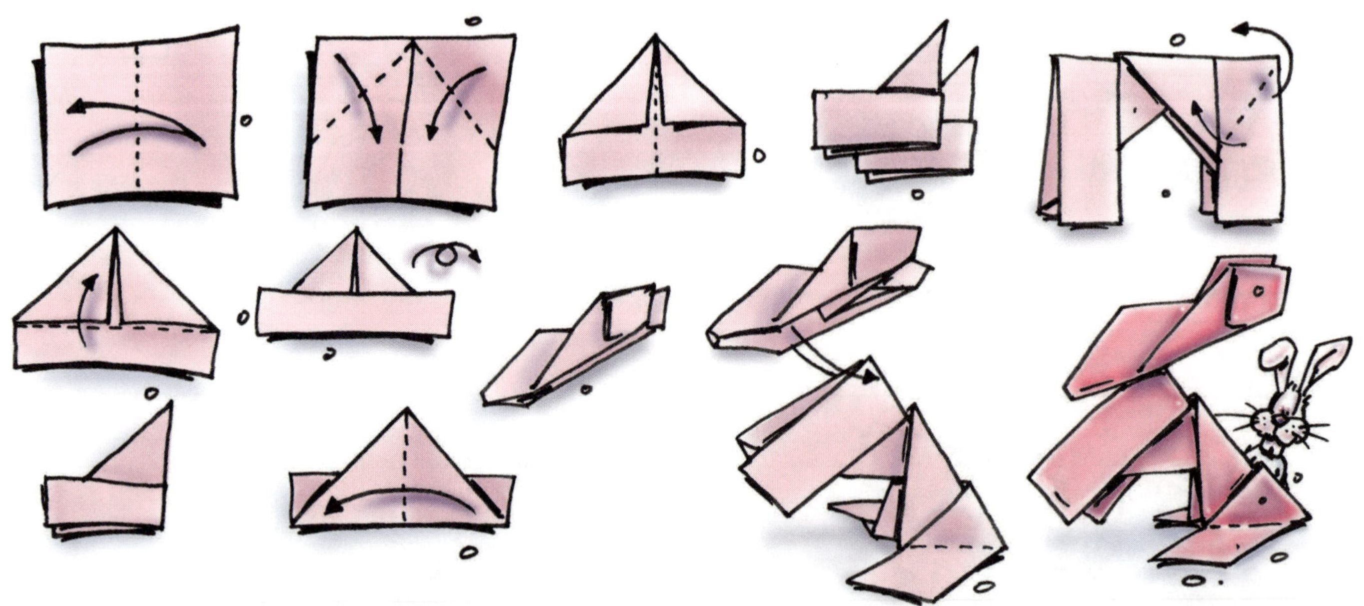

Word Bank

also	children	each	such	want
always	draw	small	walk	which

G Dictation

Name ___________________

Listen and write the missing words.

1. ________ ______ ______ ________
______ ______?

2. Sarah ________ brings ______ doll.

3. Those ______ ______ ________ apples.

4. ______ ______ ______ ______ ______
______ ______?

H Proofreading

One word in each set is misspelled. Fill in the oval by the misspelled word.

1. ○ allwayz ○ left ○ none

2. ○ smal ○ want ○ who

3. ○ could ○ wich ○ such

4. ○ noon ○ draw ○ allso

5. ○ water ○ paint ○ wak

6. ○ children ○ quit ○ eech

★ ○ caled ○ looked ○ praise

★ ○ party ○ luch ○ world

★ ○ wonted ○ balloon ○ knew

I Game

Name ______________________________

Follow the rabbit tracks to Pleasant Valley Retirement Center. Move one space each time you or your team spell a word correctly from this week's word list.

Remember: God sends special blessings to those who listen to His Word.

J Journaling

Make a list of people you know who might be lonely.
Label your list: **People to Cheer Up**.

A Test-Words

Name ______________________

Write each spelling word on the line as your teacher says it.

1. ______________ 6. ______________

2. ______________ 7. ______________

3. ______________ 8. ______________

4. ______________ 9. ______________

5. ______________ 10. ______________

Review

Lesson

24

B Test-Sentences

The two underlined words in each of the sentences are misspelled. Write the sentences on the lines below, spelling each underlined word correctly.

The gerl will cownt the money.

1. ______________________________

The blak dog made a lot of noiz.

2. ______________________________

In touwn there is a bigger stor.

3. ______________________________

Test-Challenge Words

Write each challenge word as your teacher says it.

Review Lesson 24

C Test-Dictation

Name ______________________

Listen and write the missing words.

1. ________ _____ __________ rain ______?

2. ________ soccer ________ ____ __________.

3. ________ ________ ________ ______ music?

D Test-Proofreading

One word in each set is misspelled. Fill in the oval by the misspelled word.

1. ◯ dor
   ◯ ear
   ◯ noon

2. ◯ around
   ◯ Lorb
   ◯ toy

3. ◯ roum
   ◯ small
   ◯ would

4. ◯ who
   ◯ house
   ◯ kow

5. ◯ boyz
   ◯ walk
   ◯ children

6. ◯ here
   ◯ cood
   ◯ soon

7. ◯ bow
   ◯ nyu
   ◯ enjoy

8. ◯ draw
   ◯ wood
   ◯ sowth

9. ◯ sutch
   ◯ zoo
   ◯ sound

☆ Test-Challenge Words

Write each challenge word as your teacher says it.

E Test-Shapes

Name ______________________

Color each marker on which the word is spelled incorrectly.

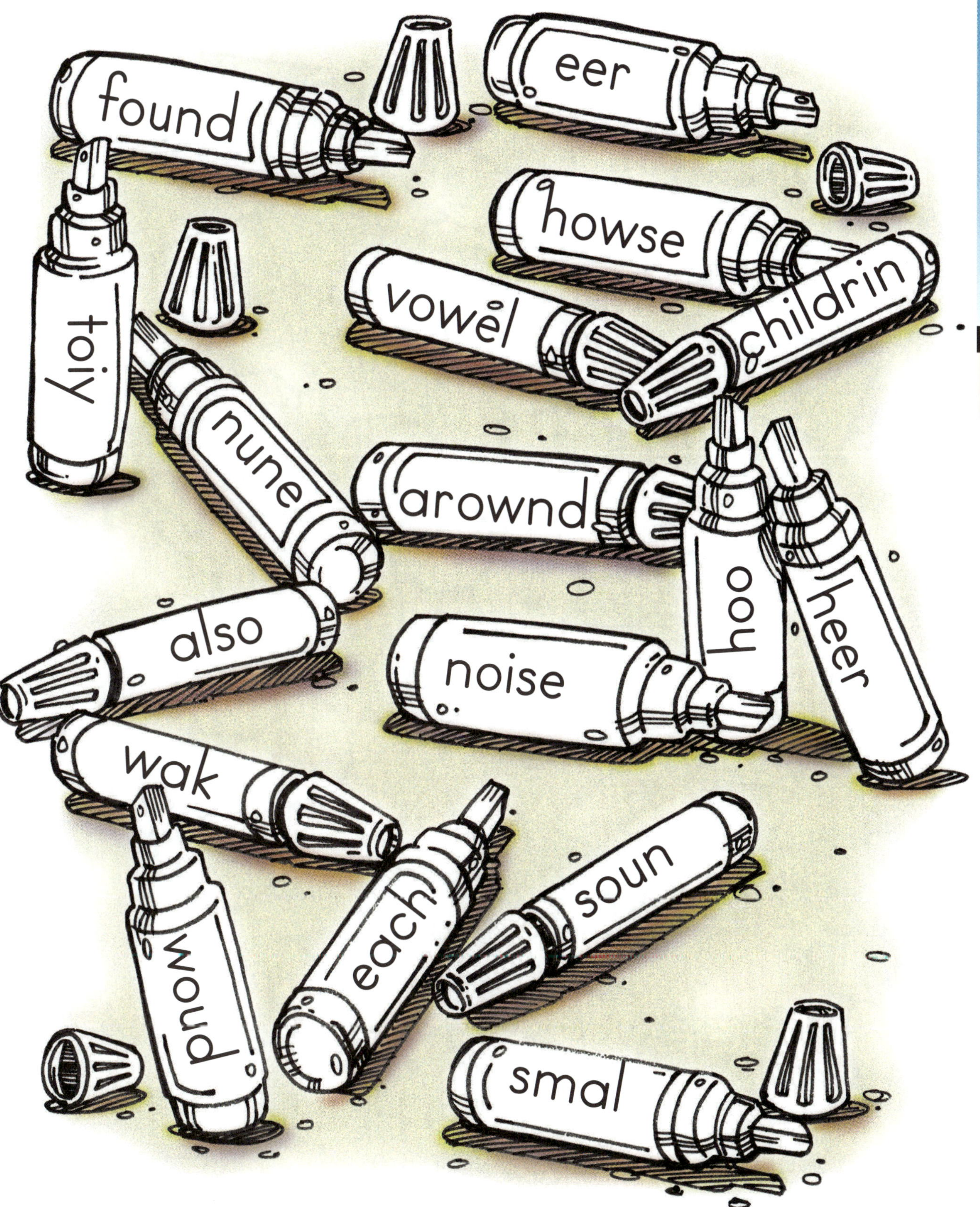

☆ Test-Challenge Words

Write each challenge word as your teacher says it.

Review

Lesson 24

F Game

Name ______________________________

Kristin shared her markers with Katelynn when completing a worksheet on geometric shapes. Use shapes as your team names for this game. Place a sticker each time you or your team spell a review word correctly.

Remember: Treat others the way you would like to be treated.

G Test-Words

Name ______________________

Write each spelling word on the line as your teacher says it.

1. ______________________ 6. ______________________

2. ______________________ 7. ______________________

3. ______________________ 8. ______________________

4. ______________________ 9. ______________________

5. ______________________ 10. ______________________

Review
Lesson
24

H Test-Sentences

The two underlined words in each of the sentences are misspelled.
Write the sentences on the lines below, spelling each underlined word correctly.

My <u>muther</u> said we could feed the <u>hors</u>.

1. ____

<u>may</u> I keep this <u>touth</u> I pulled ?

2. ____

All the <u>litle</u> beads are <u>rownd</u>.

3. ____

☆ Test-Challenge Words

Write each challenge word as your teacher says it.

I Writing Assessment

Name ______________________________

Write four sentences about a time when you helped someone.

1. ____

____

2. ____

____

3. ____

____

4. ____

____

Scripture

Matthew 7:12

Review

Lesson 24

This certificate is awarded to:

____

for practicing the following words, doing terrific spelling activities and playing great spelling games!

Date __________________________

books	food	around	boys	also
could	new	bow	door	always
dear	noon	count	enjoy	children
ear	room	cow	form	draw
full	soon	found	horse	each
hear	too	house	Lord	small
here	tooth	round	noise	such
took	use	sound	orange	walk
wood	who	south	store	want
would	zoo	vowel	toy	which
☆ looked	☆ balloon	☆ cloud	☆ before	☆ called
☆ stood	☆ knew	☆ crown	☆ important	☆ lunch
☆ year	☆ through	☆ flower	☆ voice	☆ wanted

Dear Parent,

We are about to begin a new spelling unit containing five weekly lessons. A set of ten words plus three challenge words will be studied each week. All the words will be reviewed in the sixth week.

Values, based on each Scripture listed below, will be featured in that week's lesson.

Lesson 25	Lesson 26	Lesson 27	Lesson 28	Lesson 29
dish	band	back	another	bell
finish	bend	bring	both	better
fish	blind	clock	other	dress
shoe	candy	duck	thank	funny
shop	end	hang	these	grass
should	find	milk	thick	guess
show	grand	sick	thin	mitten
shut	Indian	sing	think	pull
wash	kind	talk	those	rabbit
wish	pond	truck	thought	still
☆ shelf	☆ friend	☆ along	☆ brother	☆ different
☆ shoes	☆ index	☆ block	☆ father	☆ dinner
☆ short	☆ second	☆ something	☆ together	☆ letter
Luke 4:19	John 8:32	Matt. 5:47	Matt. 4:17	Luke 12:37

A Preview

Name ______________________

Write each word as your teacher says it.

1. ______________________

2. ______________________

3. ______________________

4. ______________________

5. ______________________

6. ______________________

7. ______________________

8. ______________________

9. ______________________

10. ______________________

Words with /sh/

Lesson 25

Challenge Words

 ______________________

☆ ______________________

☆ ______________________

Scripture

Luke 4:19

Words with /sh/

Lesson 25

B Word Shapes

Name ______________________________

Write each word in the correct Word Shape Boxes. Then, in the Word Shape Boxes, color the letters that spell the sound of **/sh/** in each word. Circle the words that end with the digraph **sh**.

1. dish
2. finish
3. fish
4. shoe
5. shop
6. should
7. show
8. shut
9. wash
10. wish

Challenge

Draw a Shape Box around each letter:

s h e l f   s h o e s   s h o r t

C Hide and Seek

Name ______________________________

Circle a cookie for each word you spell correctly.

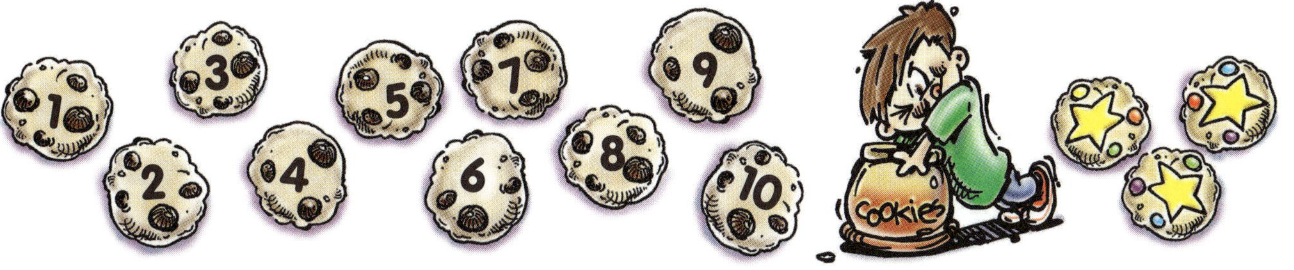

D Other Word Forms

Using the words below, follow the instructions given by your teacher.

dishes	fished	shopped	showed	washed
dished	fishing	shopping	showing	washing
finishes	ships	shorter	shuts	wishes
finished	shoe	shortest	shutting	wished
finishing	shoes	shows	washes	wishing

E Fun Ways to Spell

Initial the box of each activity you finish.

1.

Spell your words with crayon . . .

3.

Spell your words with rhythm instruments . . .

2.

Spell your words with sidewalk chalk . . .

4.

Spell your words with cotton balls . . .

F Letter Change

Name ______________________

Change the underlined letter or letters and write the spelling word on the blank.

1. __________ The d<u>a</u>sh was full of potatoes.
2. __________ The gold fis<u>t</u> swam to the top.
3. __________ I w<u>a</u>sh I could play T-ball.
4. __________ Your sho<u>d</u> string is untied.
5. __________ This shi<u>p</u> sells tapes and books.
6. __________ We <u>w</u>ould thank God.
7. __________ Matthew will s<u>l</u>ow me how.
8. __________ The back door is sh<u>o</u>t.
9. __________ We w<u>i</u>sh our hands.
10. __________ Let's f<u>am</u>ish the game now.

Word Bank

dish	fish	shop	show	wash
finish	shoe	should	shut	wish

Words with /sh/

Lesson 25

G Dictation

Name ______________________

Listen and write the missing words.

1. _______ ___ _______ ______ window?

2. Tony ______ _______ ______ _____ gift.

3. Please _______ _____ _______ _____

_______ ______ _______.

4. _______ polishing ____ ______.

H Proofreading

One word in each set is misspelled. Fill in the oval by the misspelled word.

1. ◯ air
   ◯ shood
   ◯ shut

2. ◯ dark
   ◯ pay
   ◯ wosh

3. ◯ shopp
   ◯ form
   ◯ dish

4. ◯ ready
   ◯ wish
   ◯ shooe

5. ◯ bear
   ◯ tooth
   ◯ sho

6. ◯ finsh
   ◯ fish
   ◯ children

★ ◯ heart
  ◯ shefl
  ◯ lunch

★ ◯ shotr
  ◯ voice
  ◯ large

★ ◯ important
  ◯ flower
  ◯ shooz

I Game

Name ______________________________

Run the bases in a game of T-ball while Stephen umpires. Move one space each time you or your team spell a wordcorrectly from this week's word list.

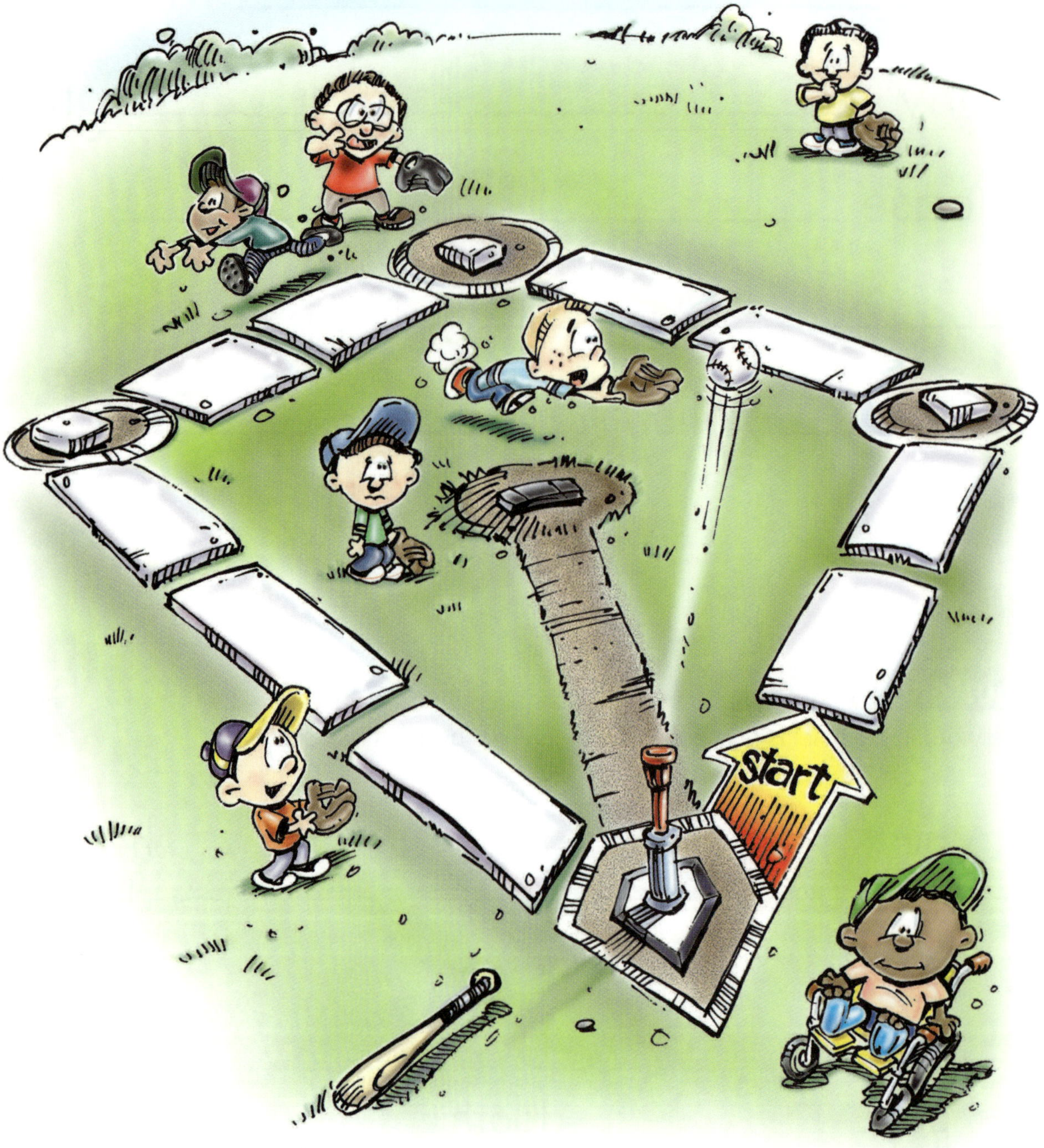

start

Remember: Call out to God and ask Him for His blessing.

J Journaling

Write a thank-you letter to someone who has been a blessing to you.

A Preview

Name ______________________

Write each word as your teacher says it.

1. ______________________

2. ______________________

3. ______________________

4. ______________________

5. ______________________

6. ______________________

7. ______________________

8. ______________________

9. ______________________

10. ______________________

Challenge Words

 ______________________

 ______________________

☆ ______________________

Scripture

John 8:32

Words with /nd/

Lesson 26

B Word Shapes

Name ______________________________

Write each word in the correct Word Shape Boxes. Then, in the Word Shape Boxes, color the letters that spell the sound of **/nd/** in each word. Circle the words in which **/nd/** comes in the middle of the word.

1. band
2. bend
3. blind
4. candy
5. end
6. find
7. grand
8. Indian
9. kind
10. pond

Challenge

Draw a Shape Box around each letter:

friend   index   second

C Hide and Seek

Name ____________________

Circle a cookie for each word you spell correctly.

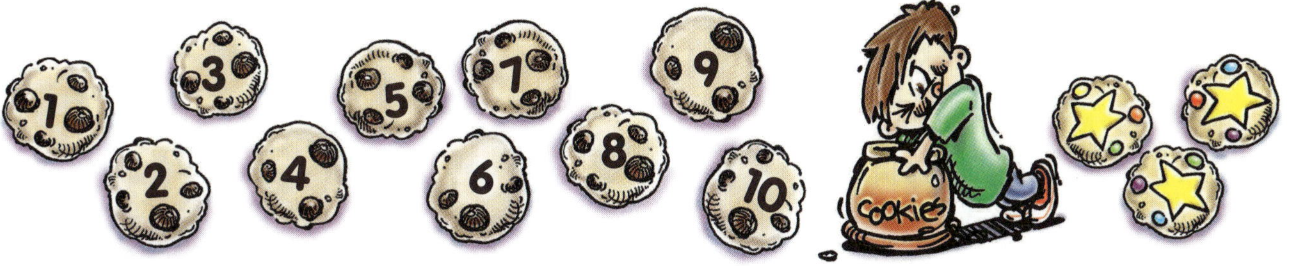

D Other Word Forms

Using the words below, follow the instructions given by your teacher.

bands	blinded	ending	kinds
banded	blinding	finds	ponds
bends	candies	friends	seconds
bending	ended	indexes	seconded

E Fun Ways to Spell

Initial the box of each activity you finish.

1. 

Spell your words with an eraser . . .

3. 

Spell your words with clapping . . .

2. 

Spell your words with paint . . .

4. 

Spell your words in damp sand . . .

F Guide Words

Name ______________________

These word pairs are Guide Words like those that appear in a dictionary. Write your spelling words on the line or lines below each set of Guide Words for the page on which they would appear. Use all the words from your Word Bank.

Word Bank

band	blind	end	grand	kind
bend	candy	find	Indian	pond

G Dictation

Name ______________________

Listen and write the missing words.

1. ___ ___ ________ _____ watch _____ marching ______.

2. Taffy ___ ______ _____ _____ ______.

3. ________ ___ ___ _______ ____ _____ ____ ____ ____ ________.

4. ______ ________ ______ ______.

H Proofreading

One word in each set is misspelled. Fill in the oval by the misspelled word.

1. ⬭ been
   ⬭ candi
   ⬭ grand

2. ⬭ podn
   ⬭ soft
   ⬭ find

3. ⬭ dand
   ⬭ show
   ⬭ plan

4. ⬭ end
   ⬭ sister
   ⬭ blinde

5. ⬭ wash
   ⬭ biend
   ⬭ kind

6. ⬭ must
   ⬭ indian
   ⬭ shoe

★ ⬭ frend
   ⬭ through
   ⬭ shoes

★ ⬭ crown
   ⬭ shelf
   ⬭ endex

★ ⬭ secund
   ⬭ beside
   ⬭ short

Words with /nd/

Lesson 26

I Game

Name ______________________________

Tony is getting treated to ice cream after his baseball game. Lead the way to the ice cream shop by moving one space each time you or your team spell a word correctly from this week's word list.

START

Remember: God sets us free to live and love others.

J Journaling

Make a list of people whom you love.
Label the list: **People I Love**.

A Preview

Name ____________________

Write each word as your teacher says it.

1. ____________________
2. ____________________
3. ____________________
4. ____________________
5. ____________________
6. ____________________
7. ____________________
8. ____________________
9. ____________________
10. ____________________

Challenge Words

 ____________________

★ ____________________

★ ____________________

Scripture

Matthew 5:47

Words with /ng/ or /k/

Lesson 27

B Word Shapes

Name ______________________________

Write each word in the correct Word Shape Boxes. Then, in the Word Shape Boxes, color the letter or letters that spell the sound of **/ng/** or **/k/** in each word. Circle the word which has a silent **l**.

1. back 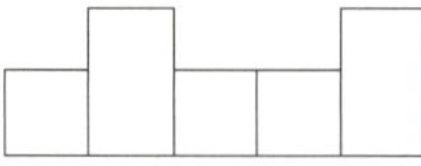
2. bring 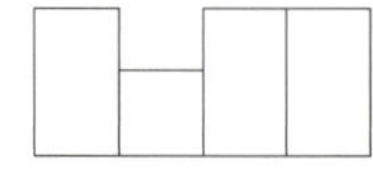
3. clock 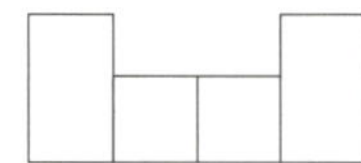
4. duck 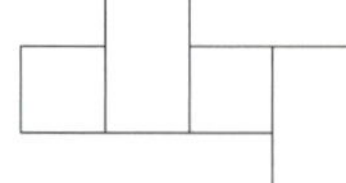
5. hang 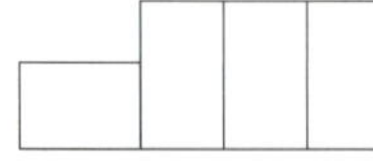
6. milk 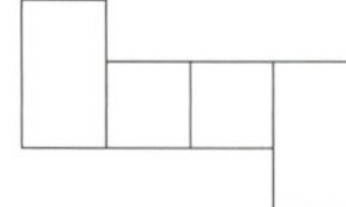
7. sick 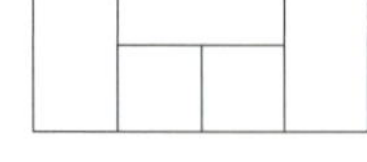
8. sing 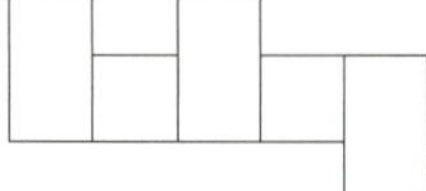
9. talk 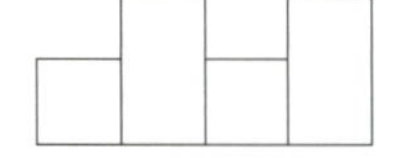
10. truck

Challenge

Draw a Shape Box around each letter:

a l o n g　　　b l o c k　　　s o m e t h i n g

C Hide and Seek

Name ____________________

Circle a cookie for each word you spell correctly.

D Other Word Forms

Using the words below, follow the instructions given by your teacher.

backs	brought	hangs	sickest	talking
backed	bringing	hung	sickly	talker
backing	clocks	hanging	sings	trucks
backer	clocked	hanger	sang	trucked
blocks	clocking	milks	singing	trucking
blocked	ducks	milked	singer	trucker
blocking	ducked	milking	talks	
brings	ducking	sicker	talked	

E Fun Ways to Spell

Initial the box of each activity you finish.

1.

Spell your words with puzzles . . .

2.

Spell your words on a paper chain . . .

3.

Spell your words out loud . . .

4.

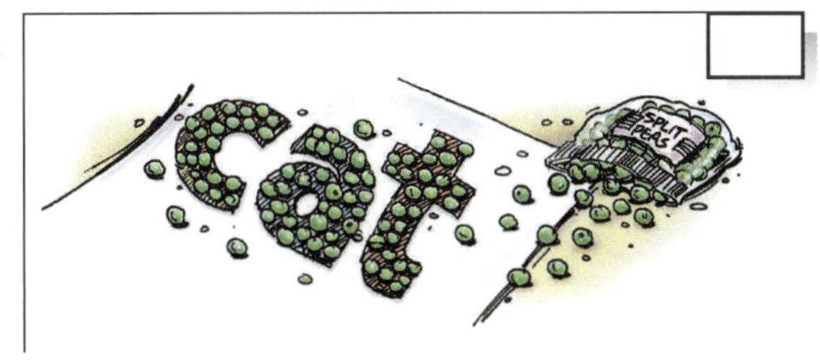

Spell your words with split peas . . .

F Word Change

Name ______________________

Write spelling words in place of the underlined words.

1. Setsuko likes to say words to her cousins. __________
2. They will fasten a banner on the wall. __________
3. Everyone will carry in birthday presents. __________
4. Father will come through the not in front door. __________
5. The thing that tells time just struck six o'clock. __________
6. I think I hear his bigger than a car coming now. __________
7. Bend down behind the couch to surprise him! __________
8. We'll make music with voices "Happy Birthday to You." __________
9. Do you want a glass of white drink with your cake? __________

Word Bank

back	clock	hang	sick	talk
bring	duck	milk	sing	truck

G Dictation

Name ____________________

Listen and write the missing words.

1. ______ ______ ______ ______ drives ______ ______ ______.

2. ______ ______ preened ______ feathers ______ ______ ______.

3. ______ ______ ______ ______ ______ ______ ______ wall.

H Proofreading

One word in each set is misspelled. Fill in the oval by the misspelled word.

1. ◯ finish ◯ truck ◯ sinj

2. ◯ hayg ◯ shop ◯ purple

3. ◯ clok ◯ car ◯ milk

4. ◯ plays ◯ sik ◯ its

5. ◯ nest ◯ tok ◯ bring

6. ◯ gone ◯ duck ◯ dack

★ ◯ lunch ◯ friend ◯ alonj

★ ◯ sumthing ◯ second ◯ cloud

★ ◯ knew ◯ blok ◯ index

I Game

Name ______________________________

Setsuko and her mother picked up the rolls of paper towels for the woman who said unkind things about them. You can help too by coloring one roll each time you or your team spell a word correctly from this week's word list.

Remember: Be kind — even to those who do not like you.

J Journaling

Draw a picture of Jesus and you together. Underneath the picture write how you can show your love for others.

A Preview

Name ____________________

Write each word as your teacher says it.

1. ____________________

2. ____________________

3. ____________________

4. ____________________

5. ____________________

6. ____________________

7. ____________________

8. ____________________

9. ____________________

10. ____________________

Challenge Words

 ____________________

 ____________________

☆ ____________________

Scripture

Matthew 4:17

B Word Shapes

Name ______________________

Write each word in the correct Word Shape Boxes. Then, in the Word Shape Boxes, color the letters that spell the sound of /th/ or /th/ in each word.

1. another
2. both
3. other
4. thank
5. these
6. thick
7. thin
8. think
9. those
10. thought

Challenge

Draw a Shape Box around each letter:

brother father together

C Hide and Seek

Name ______________________________

Circle a cookie for each word you spell correctly.

D Other Word Forms

Using the words below, follow the instructions given by your teacher.

brothers	thanks	thinner
brotherly	thicker	thinnest
fathers	thickest	thinly
others	thickly	thoughts

E Fun Ways to Spell

Initial the box of each activity you finish.

1.

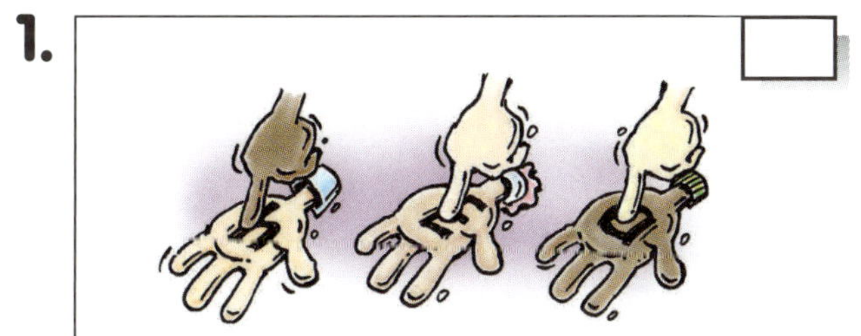

Spell your words in your classmate's hand . . .

2.

Spell your words with paper cups . . .

3.

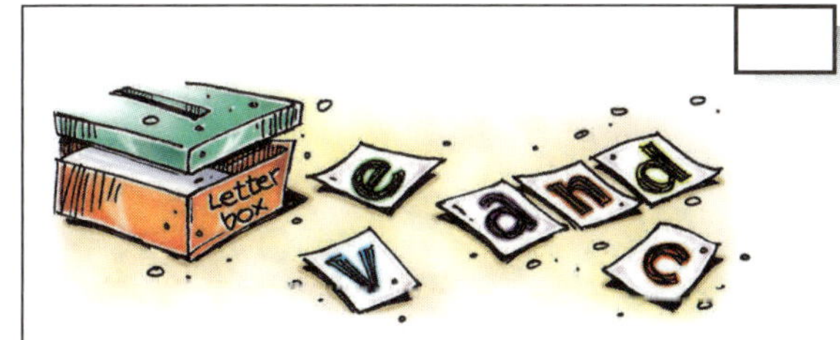

Spell your words out of the letter box . . .

4.

Spell your words with shaving cream . . .

F Rhyme Time

Name ______________________

Write spelling words from the Word Bank that rhyme with each word below:

1. win, ____________

2. mother, ____________, ____________,

★ ____________

3. hose, ____________

4. bank, ____________

5. stick, ____________

6. fought, ____________

7. sink, ____________

8. growth, ____________

9. cheese, ____________

★ bother, ____________

★ weather, ____________

Word Bank

another	other	these	thin	those	★ brother	★ together
both	thank	thick	think	thought	★ father	

G Dictation

Name ________________

Listen and write the missing words.

1. _______ _______ _______ _______

_______ blankets.

2. Setsuko _______ _______ dresses

_______ pretty.

3. _______ _______ _______ cookie.

4. ___ ___ ___ ___ ___ ___ ___.

H Proofreading

One word in each set is misspelled. Fill in the oval by the misspelled word.

1. ○ candy
   ○ theez
   ○ clock

2. ○ anuther
   ○ Indian
   ○ thank

3. ○ sick
   ○ fish
   ○ thoze

4. ○ thick
   ○ thout
   ○ blind

5. ○ back
   ○ uther
   ○ thin

6. ○ bothe
   ○ should
   ○ think

★ ○ something
  ○ bruther
  ○ block

★ ○ fother
  ○ obey
  ○ along

★ ○ don't
  ○ togethr
  ○ second

I Game

Name ______________________________

Place a game piece over each word your teacher says and spells. If the word appears on your card more than once, place a game piece over only one of the words. When you get five game pieces in a row, raise your hand and say, "Spelling is fun!"

		FREE		

Remember: Turn from your own way and go God's way.

J Journaling

Make a list of things you should turn away from. At the bottom of your list, write a note asking Jesus to help you.

A Preview

Name ______________________

Write each word as your teacher says it.

1. ______________________
2. ______________________
3. ______________________
4. ______________________
5. ______________________
6. ______________________
7. ______________________
8. ______________________
9. ______________________
10. ______________________

Challenge Words

 ______________________

★ ______________________

★ ______________________

Scripture

Luke 12:37

B Word Shapes

Name ______________________________

Write each word in the correct Word Shape Boxes. Then, in the Word Shape Boxes, color the double consonants in each word. Circle the words that have two syllables.

1. bell
2. better
3. dress
4. funny
5. grass
6. guess
7. mitten
8. pull
9. rabbit
10. still

Challenge

Draw a Shape Box around each letter:

d i f f e r e n t   d i n n e r   l e t t e r

C Hide and Seek

Name ______________________________

Circle a cookie for each word you spell correctly.

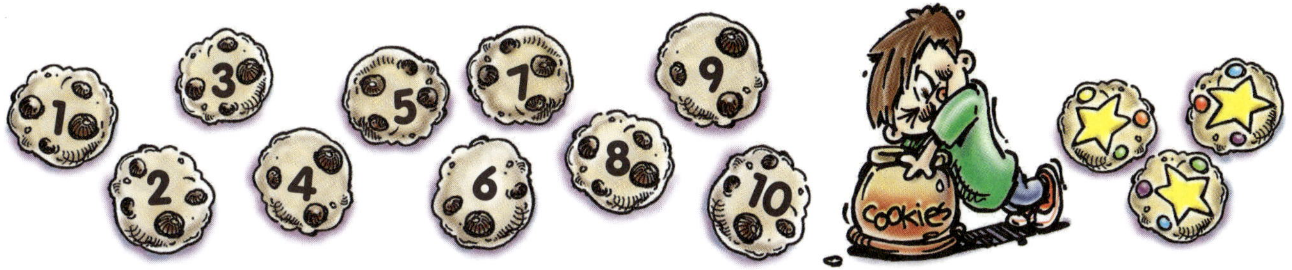

D Other Word Forms

Using the words below, follow the instructions given by your teacher.

bells	dressing	guesses	mittens	stiller
best	undress	guessed	pulls	stillest
dinners	funnier	guessing	pulled	
dresses	funniest	indifferent	pulling	
dressed	grasses	letters	rabbits	

E Fun Ways to Spell

Initial the box of each activity you finish.

1. 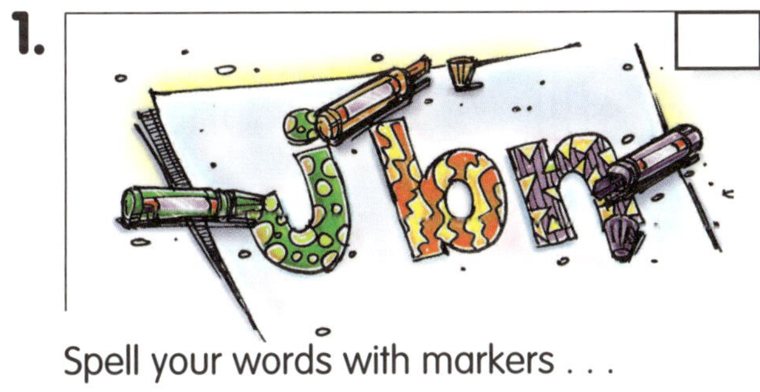

Spell your words with markers . . .

2. 

Spell your words with letter tiles . . .

3. 

Spell your words with snapping . . .

4. 

Spell your words with finger paint . . .

F Sentence Order

Name ______________________________

Write each set of word groups in order to complete a sentence.
Circle your spelling words.

looked ▪ Dad ▪ in ribbons. ▪ funny

1. ______________________________

rope to ▪ the bell. ▪ ring ▪ Pull the

2. ______________________________

the mitten ▪ I guess ▪ is lost.

3. ______________________________

grass. ▪ eats ▪ The rabbit ▪ fresh

4. ______________________________

had better ▪ this dress. ▪ Rosa ▪ wear

5. ______________________________

and proud. ▪ stood still ▪ The buck

6. ______________________________

Word Bank

bell	dress	grass	mitten	rabbit
better	funny	guess	pull	still

G Dictation

Name ______________________________

Listen and write the missing words.

1. _____ _____ _____ ate _____ _____.

2. _____ _____ _____ _____ _____

_____ _____ wagon.

3. _____ _____ _____ _____ _____ _____.

4. _____ _____ _____ _____ _____

_____ _____.

H Proofreading

One word in each set is misspelled. Fill in the oval by the misspelled word.

1. ○ another
   ○ grass
   ○ beter

2. ○ kind
   ○ these
   ○ dres

3. ○ funy
   ○ bell
   ○ shop

4. ○ those
   ○ gess
   ○ dish

5. ○ hang
   ○ rabit
   ○ dress

6. ○ end
   ○ pull
   ○ stil

★ ○ difrent
  ○ balloon
  ○ together

★ ○ father
  ○ wanted
  ○ leter

★ ○ brother
  ○ shelf
  ○ dinnr

I Game

Name ______________________

Rosa is getting ready to visit her uncle and aunt on their farm. Help her pack by moving one space each time you or your team spell a word correctly from this week's word list.

Remember: Jesus has great plans for you!

J Journaling

Write about a time you went somewhere special that you really enjoyed.
Write what you think it will be like to be with Jesus.

A Test-Words

Name ______________________

Write each spelling word on the line as your teacher says it.

1. ______________ 6. ______________

2. ______________ 7. ______________

3. ______________ 8. ______________

4. ______________ 9. ______________

5. ______________ 10. ______________

Review Lesson 30

B Test-Sentences

The two underlined words in each of the sentences are misspelled. Write the sentences on the lines below, spelling each underlined word correctly.

<u>Sevin</u> men played trumpets in the <u>badn</u>.

1. ______________________________

We saw a <u>wite</u> <u>rabitt</u> in the woods.

2. ______________________________

Mom <u>maed</u> this chewy <u>candi</u>.

3. ______________________________

☆ Test-Challenge Words

Write each challenge word as your teacher says it.

Review

Lesson **30**

C Test-Dictation

Name ______________________

Listen and write the missing words.

1. ______ ______ ______ ______ stick?

2. ______ ______ ____ ______ ______.

3. ______ ______ ______ ____ ______ ______

____ ______ street.

D Test-Proofreading

One word in each set is misspelled. Fill in the oval by the misspelled word.

1. ⬭ thik
⬭ duck
⬭ these

2. ⬭ truck
⬭ gras
⬭ sick

3. ⬭ uther
⬭ those
⬭ odd

4. ⬭ guess
⬭ thank
⬭ funy

5. ⬭ finnish
⬭ blind
⬭ odd

6. ⬭ pond
⬭ bak
⬭ show

☆ ⬭ still
⬭ talk
⬭ dres

☆ ⬭ shoo
⬭ shop
⬭ should

☆ ⬭ find
⬭ think
⬭ clok

☆ **Test-Challenge Words**

Write each challenge word as your teacher says it.

E Test-Shapes

Name ______________________________

Color each picnic item on which the word is spelled incorrectly.

☆ Test-Challenge Words

Write each challenge word as your teacher says it.

F Game

Name ______________________________

At the school picnic, Rosa and others played a tag game called "Swim, Fish, Swim!" Use types of fish as your team names for this game. Place a sticker each time you or your team spell a review word correctly.

Remember: Be honest — even in the little things.

G Test-Words

Name ___

Write each spelling word on the line as your teacher says it.

1. ___
2. ___
3. ___
4. ___
5. ___
6. ___
7. ___
8. ___
9. ___
10. ___

Review Lesson 30

H Test-Sentences

The two underlined words in each of the sentences are misspelled. Write the sentences on the lines below, spelling each underlined word correctly.

There are many fisch in the Indin Ocean.

1. ___

At scool, the bel is very loud.

2. ___

Do you drink mutch mikl?

3. ___

☆ Test-Challenge Words

Write each challenge word as your teacher says it.

I Writing Assessment

Name ______________________________

Describe a time you were tempted to be dishonest. Finally, write a promise to God to be honest.

____

____

____

____

____

____

____

Scripture

Luke 16:10

Review

Lesson 30

This certificate is awarded to:

____

for practicing the following words, doing terrific spelling activities and playing great spelling games!

Date ____________________________

dish	band	back	another	bell
finish	bend	bring	both	better
fish	blind	clock	other	dress
shoe	candy	duck	thank	funny
shop	end	hang	these	grass
should	find	milk	thick	guess
show	grand	sick	thin	mitten
shut	Indian	sing	think	pull
wash	kind	talk	those	rabbit
wish	pond	truck	thought	still
★ shelf	★ friend	★ along	★ brother	★ different
★ shoes	★ index	★ block	★ father	★ dinner
★ short	★ second	★ something	★ together	★ letter

The End